GOSPEL
F⊕UNDATIONS

THE COMING RESCUE

VOL. 4 | 2 Kings–Malachi

4

From the creators of *The Gospel Project*, *Gospel Foundations* is
a six-volume resource that teaches the storyline of Scripture. It is
comprehensive in scope yet concise enough to be completed in just one
year. Each seven-session volume includes videos to help your group
understand the way each text fits into the storyline of the Bible.

ISBN 9781535915557 • Item 005805889

Dewey decimal classification: 230

Subject headings: CHRISTIANITY / GOSPEL / SALVATION

EDITORIAL TEAM

Ben Trueblood
Director, Student Ministry

John Paul Basham
Manager, Student Ministry Publishing

Andy McLean
Content Editor

Grace Pepper
Production Editor

Alli Quattlebaum
Graphic Designer

We believe that the Bible has God for its author; salvation for its end; and
truth, without any mixture of error, for its matter and that all Scripture
is totally true and trustworthy. To review LifeWay's doctrinal guideline,
please visit lifeway.com/doctrinalguideline.

To order additional copies of this resource, write to LifeWay Resources
Customer Service; One LifeWay Plaza; Nashville, TN 37234; fax 615-
251-5933; call toll free 800-458-2772; order online at LifeWay.com; email
orderentry@lifeway.com; or visit the LifeWay Christian Store serving you.

Printed in the United States of America

Student Ministry Publishing
LifeWay Resources
One LifeWay Plaza
Nashville, TN 37234

CONTENTS

ABOUT *THE GOSPEL PROJECT*

Gospel Foundations is from the creators of *The Gospel Project*, which exists to point kids, students, and adults to the gospel of Jesus Christ through weekly group Bible studies and additional resources that show how God's plan of redemption unfolds throughout Scripture and still today, compelling them to join the mission of God.

The Gospel Project provides theological yet practical, age-appropriate Bible studies that immerse your entire church in the story of the gospel, helping to develop a gospel culture that leads to gospel mission:

Gospel Story
Immersing people of all ages in the storyline of Scripture: God's plan to rescue and redeem His creation through His Son, Jesus Christ.

Gospel Culture
Inspiring communities where the gospel saturates our experience and doubters become believers who become declarers of the gospel.

Gospel Mission
Empowering believers to live on mission, declaring the good news of the gospel in word and deed.

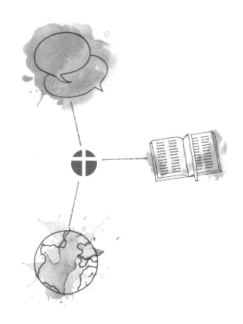

HOW TO USE THIS STUDY

This Bible-study book includes seven weeks of content for group and personal study. Each session is divided into the following components:

Introduction

Every session contains an intro option for your group time. allowing there to be a natural transition into the material for that week.

Setting the Context

This section is designed to provide the context to the biblical passage being discussed. It will help group members to not only better understand the passage under consideration for each session, but also how the biblical storyline connects between each session. It is also in this section that you will find the reference to the informational graphic for each session, once again helping students to have a deeper understanding into the storyline of Scripture.

Session Videos

Each session has a corresponding video to help tell the Bible story. After watching the video, spend some time discussing the questions provided, as well any additional questions raised by your students in response to the video.

Group Discussion

After watching the video, continue the group discussion by reading the Scripture passages and discussing the questions on these pages. Additional content is also provided on these pages to grant additional clarity into the meaning of these passages. In addition, it is in this section that you find the Christ Connection, showing students how all of Scripture points to Jesus.

Head, Heart, Hands

This section is designed to close out your group time by personally reflecting on how God's Story challenges the way we think, feel, and live as a result. Because God's Word is capable of changing everything about a person, this section seeks to spell out how each session is able to transform our Heads, Hearts, and Hands.

Personal Study

Five personal devotions are provided for each session to take individuals deeper into Scripture and to supplement the content introduced in the group study. With biblical teaching and introspective questions, these sections challenge individuals to grow in their understanding of God's Word and to respond in faith.

GOD'S WORD TO YOU

HOPE IN DARKNESS

God's plan to redeem humanity centered on Him forming a people through whom He would bring blessing to the world (Gen. 12:1-3). It would be through this people—the descendants of Abraham—that One would come to crush the head of the serpent (Gen. 3:15) and put an end to sin and death. Not only would God's blessing come through the Israelites, it would be extended to them. God had promised to care for His people, to protect them, and to be their God and Father.

But one of the ways good fathers bless is by disciplining their wayward and disobedient children. Just as God had promised to take care of Israel many times, He had also warned them of the consequences of their disobedience. But they failed to listen. Time and time again, they played the harlot with pagan gods, wanting the faithful blessings of the one true God without being faithful to Him.

God's response is found in the prophets and can be summarized by one word: repent. God called on His people to turn from their wicked ways and turn back to Him. If they did, He would receive them back, but if they did not, He would bring destruction upon them—not punitive destruction but restorative destruction. His discipline is always corrective.

And still, the people would not listen; they would not repent. So judgment came. First, it came in the form of the Assyrian army, which conquered the Northern Kingdom of Israel and hauled off its people into captivity. Afterwards, the Babylonian army destroyed the Southern Kingdom of Judah, including Jerusalem, and exiled its people.

These were dark days for God's people. They were prisoners in foreign lands, their land was occupied by pagans, and the temple lay in ruins. The blessings of God seemed more distant than ever. But though it was difficult for the people to see, God was drawing His master plan together. Toward the close of the Old Testament, God restored His people to the land, and the temple and the city of Jerusalem were rebuilt, but then God went silent. For four hundred years, the people looked, listened, and waited—the stage was set for Jesus to come and crush the serpent's head.

GOD'S FAITHFUL LOVE

*GOD FAITHFULLY PURSUES HIS PEOPLE EVEN
WHEN THEY ARE UNFAITHFUL.*

INTRODUCTION

The way a message is communicated says a great deal about the message itself and the message deliverer. Have your parents ever told you to watch your tone of voice? Have they ever commanded you not to "talk back" to them? Although the content of the message is important, the method of delivery can cause people to listen intently or turn their backs and walk away—away from the deliverer and the words he or she spoke. Even our actions, body language, and facial expressions communicate with those around us. Communicating a clear message is important, but we must also use the appropriate tone, facial expressions, and actions to accompany our words.

▶ Have you ever experienced someone delivering a message to you in such a way that you didn't want to hear them out or you didn't understand what they were saying? What happened?

In the Bible, a prophet delivered God's message to God's people. God called Hosea to be a prophet, but his method of delivery would not consist of only words— Hosea would actively demonstrate God's faithfulness to His unfaithful people. God instructed Hosea to marry a prostitute, have children with her, and continue to love and pursue her, no matter what she did or how many times she ran away from him. God actively confronted Israel's sin through Hosea's life.

SETTING THE CONTEXT

Solomon was the last king to reign over the unified kingdom of Israel. Under his son, Rehoboam, the kingdom was torn in two: Israel in the north and Judah in the south. Both nations saw many kings come and go over the next four hundred years. Some of the kings of Judah were faithful, but godly leadership was rare.

But before Israel and Judah were taken over by foreign powers, the Lord sent prophets to deliver His word—to warn the people about the future and to urge them to repent and return to Him. Truly His love was unfailing, and the prophet Hosea would demonstrate God's love for His people powerfully and visibly.

Though these prophets primarily brought warning of God's judgment, they also proclaimed God's message of love and hope. In "Seeing Jesus in the Prophets" (p. 10), we see that the rescue God had promised since Adam and Eve was coming closer to fulfillment.

SEEING
JESUS IN THE PROPHETS

Old Testament	New Testament
Hosea Pursued His Adulterous Wife; Brought Her Back from Slavery for Purity (Hos. 3)	**Jesus** Gave Himself for His Church to Make Her Holy and Blameless (Eph. 5:25-27)
Jonah In the Belly of a Great Fish Three Days and Nights (Jonah 1:17)	**Jesus** In the Heart of the Earth Three Days and Nights (Matt. 12:39-41)
Joel Prophesied of God's Spirit Poured Out on Those Who Call on Yahweh (Joel 2:28-32)	**Jesus** Pours Out His Spirit on All Who Call on Him to Be Saved (Acts 2; Rom. 10)
Jeremiah Prophesied a New Covenant for the Forgiveness of Sin (Jer. 31:31-34)	**Jesus** Shed His Blood to Establish the Covenant for the Forgiveness of Sin (Matt. 26:28)
Ezekiel Prophesied a Resurrection for God's People and a Restoration of the Land (Ezek. 37)	**Jesus** The Resurrection and the Life for All

SESSION VIDEOS

Watch this session's video, and then continue the group discussion using the following guide.

▶ What ideas or phrases stood out to you most in the video? Why?

▶ Why is Hosea's story both a vivid and appropriate illustration of God's relationship with His people?

GROUP DISCUSSION

As a group, read Hosea 1:2-9.

⭐ How are we like Gomer in our relationship with God, and God like Hosea?

▶ Why is it so easy to live as if the consequences of sin don't apply to us?

▶ What does this reveal about our nature and our relationship with God?

When God designed marriage, He instituted a relationship of such intimacy, sacrifice, and mutual love, that it would serve as a walking, talking, living, breathing illustration of the relationship between Christ and the church (Eph. 5:32).

In commanding Hosea to take an unfaithful wife like Gomer, God demonstrated the intensely personal relationship He desires with His people. Further, He illustrated just how painful and sacrificial that relationship has always been for Him as the faithful partner.

As a group, read Hosea 2:16-23.

▶ What strikes you the most in this description of God's love and commitment to His people?

⭐ What does this passage teach us about the nature of true love?

▶ How is that different from the love we readily see and experience in our culture?

If Hosea, a man, showed this kind of love and faithfulness to his wife while knowing her pattern of unfaithful behavior, then how much more must God love His people? How much more passionately does His affection burn even for those who consistently turn away from Him?

God, in His love, not only pursues us in the midst of our unfaithfulness as Hosea did with Gomer, but He promises His love to us forever. Threaded inseparably into the narrative of Hosea's marriage is God's promise of love for His own people. Just as Hosea was called to pursue and love his wife, so God has committed Himself to His people.

God's love for us is not rote and devoid of emotion—far from it. In fact, these verses along with a host of others in both the Old and New Testaments show us the deep affection God has for His people. But God's love is much deeper than that. His love, and all true love, involves willing pursuit and necessary sacrifice for the sake of the one being loved.

It's important to see in these verses that God is the One pursuing. He is leading. He is taking. He is giving. His people are the ones responding to the love God initiated. So it is with us.

As a group, read Hosea 3:1-5.

▶ What is so shocking about Hosea's actions?

⭐ How does this remind us of what God has done for us in the gospel?

The imagery is vivid and powerful:

Hosea—the abandoned but faithful husband who has every right to turn his back on his wife.

Gomer—powerless to change her situation. And then her husband, in love, paid the price for her freedom. This passage gives us a mental picture that points to the message of the gospel.

Slavery—It wasn't just that Gomer was gone; she was enslaved. Because of her lifestyle, Gomer had found herself trapped and powerless to change her own circumstances. Instead, she was at the mercy of others.

Rescuer—Hosea had every right to leave his wife, but he did not. The Lord commanded him to "go" to her because there was no way she could come to him, even if she wanted to.

Price—Hosea did not buy back Gomer on emotion, sentiment, or good intentions. He didn't stand at a distance and shout about his love for her; instead, Hosea recognized freedom doesn't come cheaply, so he went with his pockets full, willing to pay any price so that the one he loved could go free.

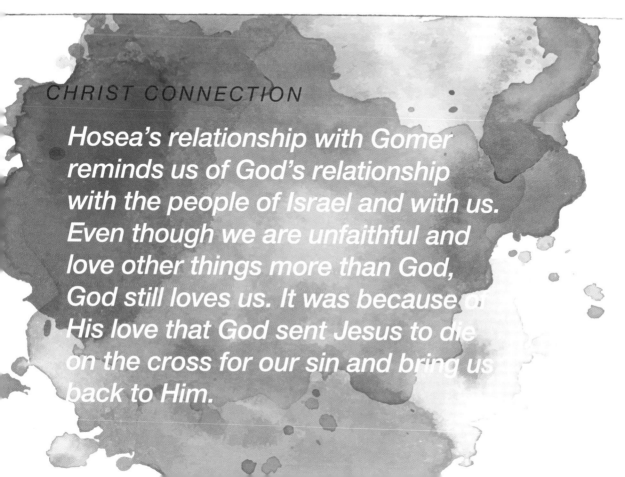

CHRIST CONNECTION

Hosea's relationship with Gomer reminds us of God's relationship with the people of Israel and with us. Even though we are unfaithful and love other things more than God, God still loves us. It was because of His love that God sent Jesus to die on the cross for our sin and bring us back to Him.

OUR MISSION

Head

Like Gomer, what are some sins that you keep running back to in your own life?

What does the story of Hosea and Gomer teach us about God's character, especially as it relates to our own unfaithfulness to Him?

Heart

How does understanding Hosea's love for Gomer help us grow in gratitude for God's love for us?

How do we, based on our usage of the word in our culture, define love? How is that different than the picture of God's love we see in Scripture?

Hands

Why do you think God asked Hosea to marry this woman? Why was it not sufficient for Hosea to deliver God's message with words alone?

What are some ways we can cultivate uncompromising devotion to God in our own lives?

⭐ **The point: God pursues us even though we are unfaithful, and He promises to love us forever.**

Hosea was given a message for the people of Israel. Only Hosea's message wouldn't just be spoken, but lived out in his own life. God instructed Hosea to remain faithful to his wife even when she was unfaithful. Through this marriage, Hosea showed the love God has for His people even when they "cheat on" Him by worshiping other gods.

▶ **Read Hosea 1:2-9.**

The Israelites had turned from God. To what did He compare their turning away in verse 2? How is turning away from God like being an unfaithful wife?

What did God tell Hosea to name his children? Based on these names, how did God view the Israelite people at the time?

Looking through this passage, we see a distinct difference in the language describing the births that would come from this marriage. Notice the description in verse 3: "she conceived and bore him a son." But then look down to verse 6 and verse 8. In both cases, the language changes: "She conceived and gave birth."

The shift in language suggests that while the first child was truly the child of Hosea, the second and third children were a result of Gomer's ongoing faithlessness. Here, then, we start to see the depth of God's command to His prophet. He was to marry an unfaithful wife and he would be reminded for years—even decades—of that unfaithfulness while caring and providing for illegitimate children.

▶ **Respond**

Consider your own relationship with God. In what ways have you been unfaithful? Journal your response.

What are some ways God has shown His love for you even when you were unfaithful.

⭐ The point: God promises rest and security.

▶ Read Hosea 2:14-23.

Explain what God did for His people, despite their rejection.

Consider God's pursuit of the people who rejected Him. What difference does it make to know that God, and not the people, repaired the relationship?

Take a minute to list the promises God made in this passage. What promises stand out to you? Why is it important to know that God will not withdraw His love from His people?

It's important to notice in these verses that there is no time limit to the love God promised. The imagery of eternity is intertwined in this poetic treatment of the love of God: We will be His people forever. We will rest in Him securely forever. He has promised and given us love, and this promise and gift will never be revoked.

▶ Respond

Just as Hosea went to Gomer when she was powerless to return to him, so Jesus came to us as the Rescuer we so desperately needed. Through His death and resurrection, He broke the chains of sin and death and brought freedom to the people of God. This freedom came not as a result of our efforts, struggling against the chains that kept us in bondage, but from One who loved us enough to come to us. Though we have been unfaithful, He faithfully gave up His life in our stead.

In what ways have you found sin to be a snare that enslaves, rather than something that frees?

How does the story of Hosea encourage you in God's pursuit of your own heart?

PERSONAL STUDY: DAY 3

✪ The point: God purchased us out of slavery to sin.

▶ Read Hosea 3:1-5.

The woman in verse 1 is assumed to be Hosea's wife, who God commanded him to marry in Hosea 1:2. She had left Hosea and was with another man.

What did God tell Hosea to do "again"? What can we learn about Hosea's relationship to his wife if God had to say "again"?

For what reason did God tell Hosea to love his wife again? What can we learn about God's love toward His people even when they choose to disobey Him?

Hosea bought back his wife for fifteen shekels of silver and some barley. The fact that he had to pay for his wife implied that she was enslaved to someone else. In order to be brought back home, she needed to be paid for.

What did Hosea promise his wife in verse 3? Would that be a hard promise to make to an adulteress? Why or why not?

▶ Respond

Think on this quote by Thomas Watson: "Till sin be bitter, Christ will not be sweet." Ask yourself: Do I see my sin as a serious problem that enslaves me or as minor mistakes?

If your sin is not a big problem to you, then Christ's payment to free you will seem unnecessary. Consider your position before God. Seek His mercy and forgiveness through the Redeemer, Jesus.

⭐ **The point: God's purchase of us required the sacrifice of His Son.**

▶ **Read Romans 8:1-4.**

In what ways were we similar to Gomer before Christ rescued us? In what ways is Hosea like Christ?

Us/Gomer   Christ/Hosea

How does Paul describe salvation in these verses?

Who made rescue and salvation possible in these verses? Why is this important to emphasize?

What made the rescue possible? Why is this important to emphasize?

▶ **Respond**

Paul sheds additional light on God's loving pursuit of us, even to the point of allowing His own Son to be condemned for our sins in order that we might be made right with Him again.

Take some time to memorize Romans 8:1-4.

⭐ **The point: A husband's love for his wife reflects God's greater love for His church.**

▶ Read Ephesians 5:22-33.

How should husbands treat their wives?

Who is the example Paul gives for husbands? Why is this important?

What is the analogy Paul also uses for a husband loving his wife? Why is this a good analogy?

According to Paul, what does marriage between a man and a woman ultimately represent and point to?

In Ephesians 5:22-33, Paul said marriage should be a picture of the relationship of Jesus and the church. Jesus is a husband who loved His bride so much that He sacrificed His life to make her pure and holy. The church receives His love and willingly chooses to love Him above all else.

▶ Respond

Hosea illustrated Paul's teaching in his own marriage. His love wasn't contingent upon his wife's faithfulness, but instead flowed from God's own love for us.

Does your understanding of marriage come more from the culture or from the Bible?

How do Paul's words here challenge your perception of marriage?

GOD'S CONTINUED PURSUIT

*GOD'S SAVING GRACE EXTENDS TO THOSE WHOM
WE MAY CONSIDER ENEMIES.*

INTRODUCTION

Have you ever tried to run away from home? There is no more famous story of running away than that of Jonah. Here was a prophet, convinced his own opinion was the correct one, and so opposed to God's direction that he ran as far away from the will and reach of God as possible. But this story is less about a man running from God than it is about God's willingness to pursue us in our disobedience.

While we tend to focus on the prophet in the story of Jonah, the main character in the Book of Jonah is God Himself. While Jonah was vindictive, God was merciful. While Jonah ran away, God pursued. While Jonah was angry, God was forgiving. God was pursuing the wicked Ninevites and also His disobedient prophet.

 Have you ever felt like you were running from God's plan and purposes? Why might we do that? What could we do to embrace God's plan and purposes instead?

SETTING THE CONTEXT

Jonah, whose name means "dove," was a prophet in the Northern Kingdom of Israel, just as Hosea was. Around that time, a new nation had risen to power— the Assyrians were brutal conquerors, and the nations lived in fear of them. This empire would be the target of Jonah's message, as God told him to go to Nineveh, a city great in number but also in importance, maybe even a capital in the Assyrian Empire.

But Jonah resisted and only delivered God's message grudgingly. In Jonah we find one reluctant to preach God's word to a particular group of people. We find a messenger who believed he knew God's message better than He who gave it. And this sets up a confrontation between God and His prophet in which Jonah would learn the truth about "God's Compassion Toward the Nations" (p. 22).

GOD'S COMPASSION TOWARD THE NATIONS

THE NATIONS	GOD'S COMPASSION	THE RESULT
All the Nations of the Earth (Gen. 12; Isa. 49)	God blessed Abraham to be a blessing to the world and raised up His Servant to restore Israel and be a light to the nations	People from every tribe, tongue, people, and nation are blessed through faith in Jesus, Abraham's descendant (Gal. 3:8; Rev. 5:9)
Rahab, a Canaanite Prostitute (Josh. 2; 6)	God granted protection to Rahab and her family from the destruction of Jericho	Rahab became the great-great grandmother of King David and an ancestor of Jesus (Matt. 1:5)
Ruth, a Moabitess (Ruth 1–4)	God provided a husband and family for Ruth from among the Israelites	Ruth became the great-grandmother of King David and an ancestor of Jesus (Matt. 1:5)
Naaman, Commander of the Army of Aram (2 Kings 5)	God healed Naaman of a skin disease through Elisha	Naaman confessed there is no God in the whole world except in Israel (2 Kings 5:15)
The Ninevites (Jonah 1–4)	God sent Jonah to preach among the Ninevites	The Ninevites believed God and repented, and God relented of their destruction (Jonah 3:5-10)

SESSION VIDEOS

Watch this session's video, and then continue the group discussion using the following guide.

▶ What ideas or phrases stood out to you most in the video? Why?

▶ Jonah is one of the most familiar stories in the Bible. How has your understanding of this story changed over time?

GROUP DISCUSSION

As a group, read Jonah 1:1-4,17.

⭐ What are some reasons we might run from the call of God?

▶ Can you share a time when you ran from the Lord?

▶ What were some of the means God used to pursue you?

You would think Jonah would be excited about an assignment like this; after all, everyone in the world knew about the Assyrians' cruelty. They were the "bullies" of the day. They were known to be brutal in their attacks and extremely oppressive when they conquered other peoples. Nineveh was described as a "great" city in verse 2, and it certainly was. A leading city of the Assyrian Empire, Nineveh was surrounded by a wall almost eight miles in length and was large enough to house 120,000 people (Jonah 3:2).

This was a chance for Jonah to confront the enemies of God's people, an opportunity for him to declare judgment—no doubt a message many of the Israelites hoped and even prayed for in their day. Jonah did "go" like God told him to, but instead of heading straight for Nineveh, he bought a ticket on a ship headed the other direction.

So why did Jonah run? Answer: Jonah knew God well enough to know God was gracious, compassionate, and full of mercy. Furthermore, he knew God was giving the Ninevites forty days of warning and inviting them to repent. Jonah could see how this would play out—he would go to Nineveh, he would speak the word of the Lord, the people would repent, and God would forgive them. No judgment. No destruction. And his hatred for the Ninevites bound him to hold back the message of God from them.

Just as God was unwilling to give up on the Ninevites, so He also was unwilling to let Jonah go his own way. God pursued Jonah even as he ran, and the means of that pursuit was a mighty storm. The storm God "hurled" into the sea was so terrible that the hardened sailors suddenly turned very religious. There are no atheists in foxholes—or on ships during a God-sized storm!

As a group, read Jonah 2:10-3:5,10.

▶ Does the response of the Ninevites surprise you? Why or why not?

★ What can we learn about evangelism from what happened in Nineveh?

▶ Who is one person in your life that you might deem beyond God's reach? How does this passage encourage you in that relationship?

Apparently, the belly of a great fish is a decent place to reevaluate your priorities. It served as that kind of environment for Jonah. Part of trusting in God's perfect fatherhood is recognizing, as a perfect Father, God exercises the right discipline at the right time. Such discipline in our lives is not evidence of His lack of care, but the proof of His love.

Ironically, Jonah found himself in the exact same position as the Ninevites. He was disobedient, living in the middle of God's discipline, and he needed to repent and ask for forgiveness. He had to preach the message to himself that God had given him for the Ninevites. And when he applied the message to himself, he was thankful for the same character of God that had driven him to such rage days earlier.

After Jonah's repentance, it is as if the story starts over again. Jonah was again given the command to go and preach to Nineveh, but this time God was more explicit in the message. Jonah didn't have any improvisational freedom in his sermon—he had to say exactly what God told him to say.

As a group, read Jonah 4:1-4,8-11.

▶ Why was Jonah so angry?

▶ What groups of people might we withhold the gospel from because we do not want them to be saved?

★ How should our prayers both for ourselves and others change in light of these passages from Jonah?

Jonah felt such animosity toward these people that he asked God to take his life rather than see them be forgiven. We should take this as a warning. We must confront prejudice and bias in our own lives, making sure that we understand our own need for God's unending mercy and grace so that in humility we can share the gospel with anyone and everyone we meet.

CHRIST CONNECTION

Jonah was a prophet who rejected God's call, ran away from his enemies, and eventually obeyed God grudgingly. Jesus followed God's call, faced His opponents, and obeyed God joyfully (Heb. 12:2). While we were still sinners, Christ died for us.

OUR MISSION

Head

Why do you think Jonah was so reluctant to speak the Word of the Lord to the Ninevites? When have you felt like Jonah—uneasy about what God was calling you to do?

Do you typically see yourself as Jonah in this story, or as the Ninevites? Why is it important for us to learn from both?

Heart

What did God want Jonah to realize with His question about Jonah's anger (Jonah 4:4)?

Have you ever felt angry because of something God did, allowed, or asked you to do? How would you respond if the Lord asked you why you were angry with Him?

Hands

Does it surprise you that Jonah's simple message was so effective? Why or why not?

What does this show us about the power of God's Word?

⭐ **The point: God pursued Jonah, even when he disobeyed.**

▶ **Read Jonah 1:1-5,15-17.**

What did God tell Jonah to do? What did Jonah do instead?

What was wrong with Jonah's plan? What is wrong with trying to escape God's will?

What made the storm stop? When someone is living in disobedience to God, what "storms" may come from their disobedience?

What did Jonah's request to be thrown overboard reveal about his faith?

What did the men on the boat think of Jonah's God after they threw Jonah into the sea? Explain.

It is possible for God to use even someone's disobedience to bring others to Himself; however, we miss out on God's blessings when we choose to disobey rather than obey.

▶ Respond

Many problems come from avoiding God's commands and running the other way. However, the lesson of Jonah is not just to obey to avoid being in trouble. The lesson of Jonah is that God's presence is everywhere—you can ignore it or you can seek it out. Consider if you are ignoring God's presence or seeking out His help in obeying His commands.

⭐ The point: God forgave Jonah and the Ninevites.

▶ ### Read Jonah 2:7–3:5.

Jonah's words in chapter 2 were spoken while he was still in the fish's belly. What did Jonah say about God?

Why do you think Jonah would speak this way of God even though God allowed him to be swallowed up by a fish? What does that say about Jonah's understanding of God?

Make a diagram of how Jonah's thought process changed from running from God to now obeying Him.

How did the people of Nineveh respond to Jonah's message?

God commanded Jonah to warn the people of Nineveh to stop their wickedness and to worship God or they would face destruction. Ironically, it was Jonah who needed to repent first. He was disobedient and sought God's forgiveness before he preached to the Ninevites.

▶ ### Respond

Consider how you receive discipline. Do you resent the person disciplining you? Challenge yourself during times of discipline to think about why you are being disciplined. What are some loving motives for someone to discipline you?

God disciplines those He loves (Heb. 12:4-11). Journal about some positive outcomes that you have experienced because of discipline.

⭐ The point: God exposed the source of Jonah's anger.

Since the people of Ninevah stopped their wickedness and sought God's forgiveness, God did not bring the destruction He had planned for them.

▶ **Read Jonah 4:1-4.**

What was Jonah's reaction to God's compassion?

Circle the words that indicate what kind of God Jonah considered Him to be.

Do you think these characteristics of God are good? Why was Jonah upset with God for being compassionate? How would you react if you were in Jonah's position?

In this passage you discover the heart of Jonah's disobedience to God: hatred of the Ninevites. What do you think lies behind our disobedience to God? Could it be a desire to elevate our wills above God's? Why or why not?

▶ **Respond**

Can you relate to Jonah? Is there anyone whom you'd rather see judgment than forgiveness? Talk honestly to God about any bitterness or resentment you may be experiencing toward someone else.

Consider the importance of forgiveness to others in the eyes of God. God willingly forgives anyone who comes to Him (John 3:16-18). How might truly knowing and understanding the love God has shown you through His forgiveness of your sins motivate you to love others?

⭐ **The point: God calls His people to grieve over their sin and return to Him in repentance.**

▶ **Read Joel 1:1-14.**

What was happening to the people of Israel?

What did Joel tell the people to do? Why is it appropriate for God's people to feel deep sadness at times?

In the past God sent locusts to invade the Egyptians (Ex. 10:1-4). In Joel 1:2-3, Joel told the people to think back to this event. Read Exodus 10:1-4 and answer: What were the people to tell their children and grandchildren about why God sent the locusts?

▶ **Read Joel 2:13-14.**

What adjectives were used to describe God? How might knowing these characteristics of God encourage us to turn from sin and turn to God?

Why is it significant that "He may turn and relent" (v. 14)? Explain.

▶ **Respond**

Does it make you sad that you have not always obeyed a gracious and loving God? Take time to honestly talk to God about your reaction to your own sin. Ask Him to give you a heart that is grieved by sin.

Who is God to you? Is He someone you talk to when you've messed up? Look back at all you've learned about God's character this week to remind yourself that God is always willing to forgive repentant people.

⭐ **The point: We reflect God in how we relate to Him and others.**

▶ Read Joel 2:18,25-32.

In verse 27, what was God teaching His people through their experience with the locusts and the eventual repayment to come? How might knowing God's purposes behind His actions help someone better understand Him and what He desires from them?

In Old Testament times, God's Spirit among the Israelites meant power, success, and military victories for the people. How did Joel describe what would happen to the people when God's Spirit came? How is that different than what they previously expected from God's Spirit?

God's Spirit came to Jesus' disciples in Acts 2:1-8. What did the Spirit enable them to do? How is this miracle exactly like what Joel spoke of?

God restored His people, Israel, and offers restoration to those who trust in Jesus as Savior. Then, God calls believers to tell others about His offer of restoration. We are accountable for sharing this gospel truth with others.

▶ Respond

Over and over again God reaffirms that He wants His people to know Him. Jesus said eternal life was knowing God and knowing Himself (John 17:3). Ask yourself: How well do I know God? What can I do today to know Him better?

GOD'S UNCOMPROMISING JUDGMENT

GOD PATIENTLY PURSUES SINNERS, BUT THOSE WHO HARDEN THEIR HEARTS WILL ONE DAY FACE JUDGMENT.

INTRODUCTION

The word pursue is commonly used to describe the desire to go after something like a college degree, a significant other, or true happiness. So, we have to shift our thinking concerning pursuit as it pertains to God—He persistently seeks after the wayward heart. This is what it means that God pursues us. God is patient with sinners (2 Pet. 3:9), but that does not mean He is inactive in their lives.

With Israel, God's pursuit involved forgiveness, rescue, faithfulness, provision, warning, and judgment. He pursues us out of His love, grace, and mercy. He is faithful to keep His promise to forgive us, and He provided salvation through His Son, Jesus. However, like Israel, many in our day also harden their hearts to God's pursuit. Those who fail to heed His warnings will face judgement.

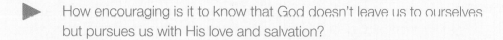 How encouraging is it to know that God doesn't leave us to ourselves but pursues us with His love and salvation?

SETTING THE CONTEXT

Through His law and His prophets, God warned His people over and over again of the consequences of abandoning their relationship with Him. Their faithlessness would bring God's judgment. God would raise up foreign leaders and armies to take away what God had given them—their land, their freedom, their prosperity, and even their temple.

Led by their kings, however, the Northern Kingdom of Israel was far too distracted by their idolatry to do what was right, as "Kings of the Divided Kingdom" (p. 34) shows, and God would eventually uphold His justice by scattering these ten tribes among the nations at the hand of the Assyrians.

Would the Southern Kingdom of Judah learn from their northern brothers? Tragically, the answer is no. King Josiah, the last bright spot among the final kings of Judah, tried every way he knew to return the people to their spiritual heritage. But after his death came a string of kings marked by idolatry and foolishness and eventually exile and destruction at the hand of the Babylonians. Yet even here, in this display of God's justice, we see how God preserved a remnant of people who would carry on the hope of His promise to make all things new through a coming Messiah.

KINGS OF THE DIVIDED KINGDOM

In the Lord's Eyes...	Did What Was Right Like David	Did What Was Right but Not Like David	Did What Was Evil	Did What Was Evil, but More Than Others
The Northern Kingdom of Israel		Jehu (but followed in the sins of Jeroboam)	Jeroboam, Nadab, Baasha, Elah, Zimri, Ahaziah, Joram, Jehoahaz, Jehoash, Jeroboam II, Zechariah, Shallum, Menahem, Pekahiah, Pekah, Hoshea	Omri, Ahab
The Southern Kingdom of Judah	Asa, Jehoshaphat, Hezekiah, Josiah	Joash, Amaziah, Uzziah, Jotham	Rehoboam, Abijam, Jehoram, Ahaziah, Ahaz, Jehoahaz, Jehoiakim, Jehoiachin, Zedekiah	Manasseh, Amon

SESSION VIDEOS

Watch this session's video, and then continue the group discussion using the following guide.

▶ What ideas or phrases stood out to you most in the video? Why?

▶ Why do you think we tend to doubt the reality of God's judgment?

GROUP DISCUSSION

As a group, read 2 Kings 17:6-13.

⭐ What can you learn about the character of God from these verses?

▶ What are some gods our hearts can drift toward, and what are some ways we can prevent this?

▶ How should the good news that God accepts us because of Christ's work give us a passionate affection for God more powerful than for any idol?

The day had finally come. As God said He would, He raised up the Assyrian Empire to destroy the Northern Kingdom of Israel. God's people were judged for their consistent and unrelenting idolatry. But even in that judgment, God was faithful to maintain a remnant of the people He had called by name. They were deported, but they lived.

As a group, read 2 Chronicles 36:11-16.

▶ How would you describe the character of Zedekiah?

▶ In what ways might we ridicule God's message today?

⭐ Why is pride so destructive in the lives of God's people?

The final downfall of Israel had been set in motion through the hardened heart of their ruler, which reflected the hardened hearts of the people. This text tells us the true source of Zedekiah's actions; he was not acting out of a sense of national pride or noble desire for independence. Instead, he was living out the natural way of his hardened heart.

All spiritual downfalls begin this way: the decline is a progression rather than a free-fall. And the first step of descent is a heart hardened to the will of God. In the hardness of Zedekiah's heart, we can see some of the warning signs that should have alerted him to impending downfall. If we watch for these kinds of signs in our own lives, they might alert us to our own hearts potentially hardening to God's will.

One of the sure signs of a hardening heart is pride. In this text we see Zedekiah's pride running out of control. In retrospect, we can look at the situation he found himself in. He was a puppet king installed by the Babylonians. His army was not large enough to counter the Egyptians, much less the Babylonians.

▶   Have you ever witnessed someone who had hardened their heart toward the will of God? What happened?

▶   Have you ever noticed yourself taking the same path? How can you guard yourself from this in the future?

As a group, read 2 Chronicles 36:17-21.

▶   Why was the destruction of God's temple so devastating for the people?

▶   Put yourself in the place of those people taken into exile. What are some of the things you might have been thinking?

⭐   Where do you see hope in these verses, even in the midst of judgment?

The people of Judah never thought the end would come. Day after day, the sun kept coming up and going down, and life went on as normal. The voices of the prophets, constantly warning about the judgment of God, faded into the background.

Perhaps the greatest tragedy of the fall of Judah was the destruction of the temple, the symbol of God's presence among His people. Surely many in Judah wondered if God had abandoned them. Yet God left His faithful witness, Jeremiah, among the people to remind them yet again of His faithful love. He had not abandoned them. Rescue would come.

CHRIST CONNECTION

God righteously punished His people for their sin, but He remained faithful to them and kept the promise He made to David to preserve a remnant and provide a king. Ultimately, God punished our sin through His Son, Jesus, and made Him our King forever.

OUR MISSION

⭕ Head

Why do you think pride comes along with hardness of heart?

What are some of the active ways we can help each other fight against pride?

♥ Heart

In your own words, what is hardness of heart? What are some of the ways you can identify if your heart is becoming hardened?

How does our response to God's Word serve as an indicator to the condition of our hearts?

✋ Hands

Why do you think God desires His people to be distinct and set apart from the world in the way that they live?

What are some ways God has called us to be distinct from the world around us?

PERSONAL STUDY: DAY 1

⭐ **The point: The kingdoms of this world oppose God's people.**

▶ **Read 2 Kings 19:8-13.**

What threat did the King of Assyria make against King Hezekiah?

Like the serpent in the garden of Eden, how did the King of Assyria try to make Hezekiah doubt God?

What hope did King Hezekiah and God's people have that the other countries did not? What set God's people apart?

▶ **Read Ephesians 6:10-13.**

According to verse 10, where do Christians get the strength to overcome the tactics of the Devil?

What specific command did Paul give to believers in verse 13?

▶ **Respond**

Think of changes you have seen in the morals of society over the last five years. Why are Christians sometimes slow to speak out or take a stand?

On what issues do you need to take a clear stance? Pray and thank God for giving you everything you need to stand firm in your faith.

⭐ **The point: God's people cry out to God for salvation and exalt His name.**

▶ **Read 2 Kings 19:14-19.**

When Hezekiah received threats from the Assyrian king, how did he respond?

In verse 15, what evidence did Hezekiah give that showed God was able to provide victory, even though all seemed lost?

Because Sennacherib was one of the most powerful kings of the time, he elevated himself above the living God and even mocked God. How does power or popularity sometimes make a person prideful?

In verses 18 and 19, how did the gods of other nations destroyed by the Assyrians differ from Hezekiah's God?

▶ **Respond**

Journal about a situation you are experiencing now or experienced in the past that seemed hopeless. Be specific—what is/was the actual problem? How did you want God to answer your prayer? Follow Hezekiah's example by placing the situation before God and taking time to focus your prayer. Be sure to ask yourself if you are praying for a selfish victory or a victory that God alone can provide.

As you deal with your difficult situation, remember the greater goal in verse 19 is that all the world may know that God alone is God. In what ways can you live as a witness to the truth that God alone is God, even through this difficult time?

⭐ **The point: God is victorious for the sake of His name and His people.**

▶ **Read 2 Kings 19:20,32-37.**

What did God say about Hezekiah's prayer (v. 20)? How did God answer Hezekiah's prayer (v. 37)?

If you were suited up for war against the Assyrians, but God promised victory without you having to fight the battle, what would be your reaction be?

How did God destroy the Assyrian army? Why is this important?

Without an army, what did King Sennacherib do after being defeated?

How and where did Sennacherib die? How does his death connect with his mockery of God?

▶ **Respond**

Think of some times you have seen God answer prayer with a clear response. What are some ways God has answered prayer in your life and how have you responded to His answers?

You might find it easier to act and plan for the here and now, but it is more important to view life from the perspective of God's greater purposes, such as bringing glory to His name and victory to His faithful followers. Why is it difficult to pray with a kingdom agenda instead of from selfish desires?

PERSONAL STUDY: DAY 4

⭐ **The point: A spiritual downfall starts with a rebellious and hardened heart.**

▶ **Read 2 Chronicles 36:11-14.**

How did King Zedekiah reign? Was he a righteous or disobedient king? Explain.

List the ways Zedekiah disobeyed in this passage.

What do you think it means that, "he … hardened his heart against returning to the LORD" (v. 13)?

God used Nebuchadnezzar, the pagan king of Babylon, to warn Zedekiah to follow the Lord (v. 13a). In what ways has God used other people or circumstances to warn you and keep you from hardening your heart against Him?

▶ **Respond**

List a few ways you can guard against hardening your heart toward the will of God. Share your list with another believer who will hold you accountable to it.

Think about this: What are a few signs that alert me when I'm falling into sin and disobedience?

For further study on what it means to have a hardened heart, read Proverbs 28:13-14; Matthew 13:14-15; and Ephesians 4:18.

PERSONAL STUDY: DAY 5

⭐ **The point: A spiritual downfall continues when we choose not to listen to the warnings and disobey the instructions in God's Word.**

▶ **Read Jeremiah 38:14-18,24-28.**

What risk did Jeremiah take in delivering God's Word to Zedekiah (v. 15)? Explain.

Describe the events that followed Jeremiah's warning. (*Hint: Compare verses 18 and 28.*)

▶ **Read 2 Chronicles 36:15-21.**

How and why did God send word to His people?

In your own words, what led to the destruction of Jerusalem and desolation of God's people (v. 16)?

What happened to the city? Where was Jeremiah when all of this took place (Jer. 38:28)?

▶ **Respond**

Pray that God will help you see His Word for what it is—wisdom and truth that is intended to be embraced and lived out.

For further study on why you should accept God's Word, read Proverbs 30:5.

GOD'S ENDURING HOPE

SALVATION COMES THROUGH THE SUFFERING OF GOD'S CHOSEN SERVANT.

INTRODUCTION

Rising to a massive 29,035 feet, Mount Everest holds the undisputed position of being the highest point on earth, rising 5½ miles above sea level. Standing on top of the majestic mountain makes climbers feel like they are on top of the world, with one foot in China and the other in Tibet. With winds exceeding 100 miles per hour and temperatures of -76 degrees Fahrenheit, even those who glimpse the unrivaled beauty of Everest's summit cannot do so for long. There is simply more beauty than any single person can appreciate surrounding this majestic treasure of the East.

Ascending from the pages of the Old Testament, Isaiah 53 stands as a spiritual Mount Everest pointing to the glory of Christ and the hope of eternal salvation. As we journey up this mountain, we encounter a prophetic picture all of us can appreciate, but none of us can exhaust. Despite being written 700 years before Jesus died on Golgotha's hill, these verses position the reader at the foot of the cross and expound on the gospel by showing us the truth of substitutionary atonement.

 What is the tallest mountain or highest elevation you have ever visited? What do you recall about that experience?

SETTING THE CONTEXT

The days were dark for the people of God. The Northern Kingdom of Israel had fallen to the Assyrians, and the Babylonians conquered the Southern Kingdom of Judah. The land God promised to Abraham and his descendants had been taken over by foreign armies, and many of the surviving Israelites had been taken into captivity.

Prior to their exile, God raised up the prophet Isaiah to warn Judah and Jerusalem to repent. He spoke about their coming destruction and gave some of the most vivid messages of hope in all of the Scriptures—messages regarding the Messiah, God's chosen Deliverer.

Another prophet, Jeremiah, also warned the people to return to God. Jeremiah bore witness to the destruction of Jerusalem, but his prophecies also told of a hope and a future God had planned for His people—"The New Covenant" (p. 46).

THE NEW COVENANT

COVENANTS OF SCRIPTURE	RECIPIENTS	COMMANDS	PROMISES/ CONDITIONS
Abrahamic Covenant (Genesis 12; 15; 17) **Permanent Covenant** (Genesis 17:7)	Abraham, Isaac, and Jacob and their descendants	• Keep the covenant • Circumcise every male	• Land • Offspring • Blessing
Mosaic (Old) Covenant (Exodus 19–24)	The people of Israel	• Keep the covenant • Obey the law	• Blessing for obedience • Curse for disobedience
Davidic Covenant (2 Samuel 7; Psalm 89) **Permanent Covenant** (2 Samuel 23:5)	David and his descendants	• Keep the covenant • Obey the law	• A great name • Stability for God's people with an eternal house, kingdom, and throne
New Covenant (Jeremiah 31:31-34; Ezekiel 36–37) **Permanent Covenant** (Ezekiel 37:26)	Believers in the Messiah	• Keep the covenant • Repentance and faith	• A new heart indwelt by God's Holy Spirit • Cleansing and forgiveness of sin • A Davidic king forever

SESSION VIDEOS

Watch this session's video, and then continue the group discussion using the following guide.

▶ What ideas or phrases stood out to you most in the video? Why?

▶ What are some ways that the messages of Isaiah and Jeremiah remind us of God's faithfulness even during times of suffering?

GROUP DISCUSSION

As a group, read Isaiah 53:4-12.

▶ What part of these verses stands out the most to you? Why?

★ What are some of the ways you see the life and death of Jesus foreshadowed in this prophecy?

▶ Why is it important for us to understand that this prophecy was written hundreds of years before the birth of Jesus?

Seeking to highlight the Servant's substitution for all people, Isaiah repeatedly used the words "we," "us," and "our" to communicate that we are the beneficiaries of His work and also guilty for these crimes. With pinpoint precision, Isaiah describes for us the events of the cross before they occurred. The Servant became a suffering substitute for us.

But why do we need a substitute? You may recall that when Adam and Eve chose to sin, humanity was left reeling under the curse of their transgression (Rom. 5:12-14). Destined to die as a result, the only hope for salvation is that our sentence of condemnation be taken away. By dying on the cross, Jesus paid the debt we owe for our inherited nature and personal actions. Rather than ignore our sin and deny His holiness, God chose to take our punishment upon Himself through the person of His Son in order to remove our sins completely.

Thus, Jesus bore our sicknesses and pain because they are a result of the curse (Isa. 53:4). God the Father pierced and crushed Him for our transgressions and iniquities so that we could enjoy peace (53:5). Because all people are like wayward sheep deserving of death (53:6; Rom. 3:23), God the Father placed the weight of our wickedness upon Christ. Jesus stood in our place and not only became sin, but also faced the consequence of sin (2 Cor. 5:21). He was cut off from the land of living because the wages of sin is death (Isa. 53:8; Rom. 6:23).

As a group, read Jeremiah 31:8-14.

Why might this prophecy have been so encouraging to God's people when they were in exile?

Why would it have been so meaningful for them to hear that God would return them to their land?

Both the Northern and Southern Kingdoms had been defeated and the people taken away as exiles. But both nations would find mercy by the grace of God, for He would one day restore them to their homeland. These verses describe how life was always meant to be, and yet they are only a shadow of the true restoration God is performing not only with Israel but also with the entire world through the gospel. One day, all will be renewed and made right.

As a group, read Jeremiah 31:31-34.

How do these verses point us to our deepest need?

Where do you see the gospel in this prophecy?

What are some of the main differences between the old covenant and the new covenant God promised in these verses?

This new covenant meets us at our deepest need because our hearts are engraved with sin—it offers the promise of a new heart indwelled by God. This new covenant gives us the amazing privilege of living in fellowship with our Creator. Through this promise, we will receive a heart that truly knows God.

From God's perspective, how fully known are we? He knows the number of hairs on our heads. He knows our deepest thoughts and motivations, and they are laid bare before Him. He knows us, in fact, better than we know ourselves. He knows our past, present, and future. God knows us completely. Fully. Without exception.

That's how well we will know God in heaven. We will see Him face to face. No matter how hard we seek after the Lord here on earth, we will always see a diluted image of Him that has been distorted by our humanity. But in heaven? No distortions. We will experience perfect and complete intimacy with God Almighty. The only way we can get there is through the gospel.

CHRIST CONNECTION

God's people had God's law but were still unable to obey Him due to the sinfulness of their hearts. Isaiah and Jeremiah prophesied about a coming day when God would forgive His people's sins and write His law on their hearts. These prophecies point to God's provision of Jesus. Through Jesus, God offers us forgiveness, and through the Holy Spirit, God enables us to obey His commands.

OUR MISSION

Head

How does the fact that these prophecies were recorded hundreds of years before the birth of Christ strengthen your faith in the reliability of Scripture?

In what ways do you often think of your relationship with God? Are you ever tempted to think of Him as no more than a cosmic butler, answering to our wishes and desires? How can you guard against this in your own life?

Heart

Worldly wisdom will tell people "trust your heart" or "believe in yourself." How do the passages in this session challenge this way of thinking?

Why is it important for us to understand we don't only commit sins, but are sinful in nature? How does this knowledge impact the way you understand the effects of the gospel?

Hands

How has this session encouraged and challenged you when it comes to your own relationship to God?

How has this session encouraged and challenged you when it comes to reflecting God to those around you?

PERSONAL STUDY: DAY 1

⭐ **The point: Jesus was an unlikely king from the line of David.**

What would it be like to meet a king? If you had the chance to talk with a king, what would you want to know about his life?

▶ **Read Isaiah 11:1.**

What images come to mind when you read the words "grow," "stump," "branch," "roots," and "fruit"?

What do you think believers are supposed to understand about Jesus based on the language Isaiah used?

Read 1 Samuel 17:12. Why do you think it's important that Jesse was mentioned in both of these passages?

God promised to build an eternal house for David. How was this promised fulfilled in Jesus?

▶ **Respond**

The Israelites were impatient and desired to have a king like all the other nations and were not satisfied with God being their king. As a result, Israel had a series of bad earthly kings.

Describe a situation in which you were tempted to be impatient with God and took matters into your own hands instead of trusting Him. Then, think about some alternate outcomes if you had waited on God's timing.

⭐ The point: Jesus is a Spirit-filled king.

▶ Read Isaiah 11:2.

This verse says the Messiah will have wisdom and understanding. What are the differences between those two things?

Wisdom

Understanding

Why does this passage place "counsel" and "strength" together? In what ways does Jesus show both Spirit-led counsel and strength?

Does having knowledge of the Lord cause us to fear Him?

List a few situations in which Jesus exhibited great knowledge and fear of the Lord.

What does this passage demonstrate about a Spirit-led life? How should this knowledge influence believers?

▶ Respond

According to Isaiah 11:2, certain characteristics naturally flowed from Jesus as a result of the Spirit of the Lord resting upon him. Even though we are still in the process of becoming like Jesus (sanctification), the Holy Spirit does dwell inside of believers. Certain characteristics should be present in our lives if we have the Spirit.

Jot down three challenges you are currently facing. Under each situation, describe how you are tempted to deal with them and then how you might deal with them differently in light of today's passage.

For the further study on a Spirit-led life, read Galatians 5:22-23.

PERSONAL STUDY: DAY 3

⭐ **The point: Jesus is a king who brings God's justice.**

▶ Read Isaiah 11:3-5.

We often judge by what we hear and see. According to verse 3, how does God execute judgment differently?

List the two specific types of people for whom God would execute justice.

Why do you think God directed His attention to those specific types of people?

Summarize what kind of king Jesus will be.

How should this motivate us to treat the poor and oppressed of the world?

▶ Respond

Now, on a note card, list a few ways you can help others come to know the freedom they can experience through Christ.

Check out organizations like The International Justice Mission, the A21 Campaign, Compassion International, and Cure International for more information on ways you can get involved in social justice today.

⭐ **The point: Jesus is a servant who was despised and rejected.**

▶ **Read Isaiah 52:13–53:3.**

How was Jesus a servant? How does this affect the way we live today?

How do you think the Israelites responded to Isaiah's prophecy of a Servant, rather than a military conqueror?

List three of Isaiah's prophecies in these verses and how Jesus fulfilled each one.

Prophecy	Fulfillment

In what ways was Jesus despised and rejected at the cross?

Why did God send Jesus to suffer? Explain.

▶ **Respond**

Think of some ways you can serve people today and show God's love. Set a reminder on your phone or jot down a reminder on a sticky note to help you remember to serve others today.

For further study on the character and actions of the Servant, read Isaiah 42:1-4.

⭐ **The point: Jesus is a servant who was pierced and crushed for our sins.**

▶ Read Isaiah 53:4-12.

In what ways did Jesus carry the sickness and pain of people?

Name some blessings that people receive because Jesus was pierced and crushed (v. 5).

According to verse 6, how are people like wayward sheep?

When Jesus, an innocent man, did not defend Himself against His accusers, what message did that send regarding His role on earth?

▶ Respond

What Jesus did on the cross was not an act of weakness but a display of authority and power. Pray and thank God for being a servant.

On a clean sheet of paper, write down any sin that comes to mind. Circle the sins that you struggle with the most. Remember that Jesus took on all the ugliness of our sin on the cross.

List some reasons why a relationship with Jesus was/is unattractive to you. Beneath that, describe the ways the realization of Jesus taking on the weight of your sin changed your perspective or desire to serve Him.

GOD'S CONTINUED STRENGTH

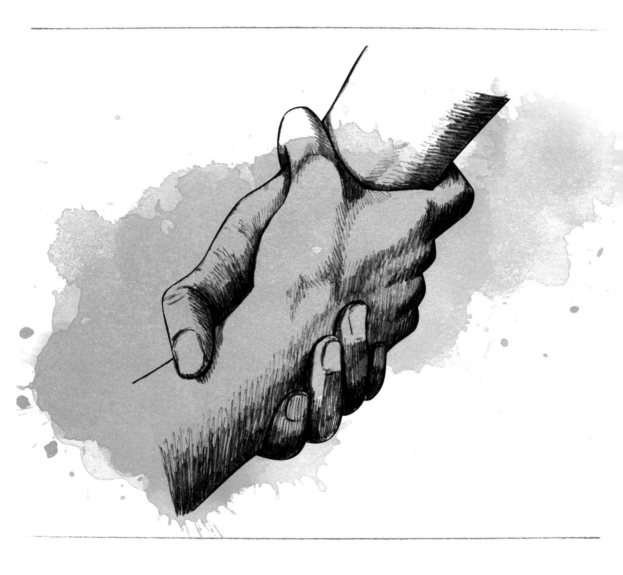

GOD GLORIFIES HIMSELF THROUGH THE RESCUE OF THOSE WHO TRUST HIM.

INTRODUCTION

Have you ever played a game of Bible trivia or word association, in which you match well-known people and events? Here are a few examples:

Adam and _____. Cain and _____. Noah and the _____. Jacob and _____. Samson and _____. David and _____. Sodom and _____.

And what do you think of when you hear the name Daniel? Most likely, you think of a "lions' den." Now we've arrived at the most famous story in the book of Daniel. This man of God ruled with wisdom under Nebuchadnezzar (5:12). He had a good reputation and was known to be a man of character, filled with the Spirit of God. No one had anything negative to say about him, even into the reign of Belshazzar, the last Babylonian king. Even king Darius shared their opinion and appointed Daniel to a position of significant leadership.

Suddenly, Daniel faced a major test of faith. Within a few short days, we see a faithful 80-year-old man thrown into a pit with ravenous lions ready to tear him apart. Why? Because he wouldn't stop praying.

▶ What do you know about the story of Daniel in the lions' den? Why do you think this particular story has become so well known in culture and in the church?

SETTING THE CONTEXT

The prophet Jeremiah told the people that God had not abandoned them; in fact, he reminded them that God had plans for them, plans to give them a hope and a future (Jer. 29:11). But he also told them that their captivity would last seventy years. In this foreign land, they were to go about regular lives, building houses, planting gardens, getting married, and praying regularly that the land they were in would thrive.

Some notable deported Hebrews, Daniel and his friends, chose not to cower in fear of the foreigners. These Hebrews excelled before both God and man, and they remained faithful to their God, even in the midst of great adversity. Therefore, God elevated them to important points of leadership in Babylon.

"Daniel's Life" (p. 58) recounts some ways these Hebrews demonstrated their faith. Shadrach, Meshach, and Abednego refused to bow to Nebuchadnezzar, the conqueror of Jerusalem, though it meant they would be thrown into a furnace of fire.

57

DANIEL's *LIFE*

REIGN OF NEBUCHADNEZZAR

- Daniel was exiled from Judah, taken to Babylon to serve in the king's palace (1:3-6)
- Chose not to defile himself with the king's meat and wine (1:8-16)
- Excelled in counseling the king in every matter of wisdom (1:19-20)
- Told and interpreted the king's dream by the wisdom of God (2:26-45)
- Promoted to ruler over the entire province of Babylon (2:48)
  - Shadrach, Meshach, and Abednego refused to worship the king's statue; thrown in the furnace but saved by God (3:8-30)
- Interpreted the king's dream regarding God's punishment for his pride (4:19-27)

REIGN OF BELSHAZZAR

- First Year: Daniel's vision of four beasts representing four kings of the earth (7:1-28)
- Third Year: Daniel's vision of a ram and a goat representing two kings (8:1-27)
- Called before the king and interpreted the handwriting on the wall (5:13-31)
- Promoted to third ruler in the kingdom (5:29)

REIGN OF DARIUS THE MEDE/ CYRUS THE PERSIAN

- First Year: Daniel received understanding about Jeremiah's 70 years of exile (9:1-27)
- Third Year: Daniel's vision of a glorious Man and the last days (10–12)
- Appointed as an administrator over the satraps of the kingdom (6:1-2)
- Ignored the king's edict and prayed to God; accused by his enemies (6:10-15)
- Thrown in the lions' den but saved by God (6:16-23)
- Told in a vision to go until the end and await his resurrection at the end of the days (12:13)

SESSION VIDEOS

Watch this session's video, and then continue the group discussion using the following guide.

▶ What ideas or phrases stood out to you most in the video? Why?

▶ Why do you think the temptation to compromise our commitment is so great during times of adversity?

GROUP DISCUSSION

As a group, read Daniel 6:6-15.

⭐ How would you describe Daniel?

▶ Does he remind you of any other person from Scripture?

▶ What does it tell us about Daniel that these men were able to lay this trap for him?

Daniel was the model worker and employee. Daniel's walk with God was consistent. When emergencies or crises presented themselves, Daniel was already prepared to meet and handle them. His daily communion with God shaped his character. He knew who he was and what was required of him.

The officials knew if they wanted Daniel gone, they had to use his integrity against him. By manipulating Darius into making an irreversible decree, the officials hoped to trap Daniel in an act of disobedience to the king. Their goal was not to see Daniel demoted; their goal was to see Daniel dead.

When Daniel found out Darius signed an edict honoring himself as the exclusive deity of the empire, what did he do? He did what he had always done—he obeyed God rather than man. He continued a pattern of spiritual devotion that had marked his life for years, a pattern his enemies knew well. He went to his home, upstairs to the place of prayer, where the windows were open toward Jerusalem. He then got down on his knees and prayed three times daily, as he had always done.

GROUP DISCUSSION *CONT.*

As a group, read Daniel 6:16-24.

▶ How would you describe Darius?

⭐ What must Daniel have believed to be true about God to remain faithful?

These evil men had counted on Daniel to be true to His God. Daniel knew that past faithfulness would be no substitute for present faithlessness. Indeed, the past had simply prepared him for the present and the future. One's character is not forged in the moment of adversity but is revealed in the moment of adversity.

Most likely, Daniel knew about his friends, Shadrach, Meshach, and Abednego and their experience in the fiery furnace. Showing the same kind of conviction, Daniel did not falter in his faith. Just as his friends had told King Nebuchadnezzar that their allegiance to God trumped every idol, Daniel demonstrated to Darius that his fidelity to God was not subject to debate.

Much to his regret, Darius then commanded that Daniel be thrown into the lions' den. The den was probably a pit with an opening at the top. The king also sealed Daniel's tomb with the royal signet rings. We can only imagine the joy of these officials when this took place.

As a group, read Daniel 6:25-27.

▶ What is encouraging to you about the proclamation from the king?

⭐ How does this proclamation reveal both God's mission and His glory?

As Darius approached the lions' den he cried out for Daniel, wondering if he might still be alive. Suddenly, Daniel spoke, making it clear that no harm had come upon him. God had supernaturally intervened to shut the mouths of the lions, and Daniel made sure all who were present knew this truth. Daniel was brought out of the lions' den, and the king sent those who maliciously accused Daniel to face the lions themselves.

We see how God used this entire story to show His power to the pagan world. Darius was clearly impacted by God's miraculous deliverance of Daniel. His declaration accomplishes at least two important purposes: It recognizes the greatness, even the superiority, of Israel's God, and it cancels out the irrevocable edict of verses 6-9. This is an amazing example of how God can even use unbelievers to proclaim His glory. As Proverbs 21:1 says, "A king's heart is like streams of water in the Lord's hand: He directs it wherever He chooses."

CHRIST CONNECTION

Daniel faithfully trusted and obeyed God even at risk of his life. God rescued Daniel from death and used him to advance His kingdom. Like Daniel, Jesus faithfully trusted and obeyed God, but unlike Daniel, Jesus was not spared from death. Jesus died and was resurrected to advance the kingdom of God.

OUR MISSION

◯ Head

How does this account give you a different perspective on personal trials, allowing you to step back and see the bigger picture of God's work?

Share about a time when God used a difficult period in your own life to point others to Himself.

♥ Heart

When Daniel refused to obey the king's edict, what statement did it send to the rest of the world? What are some areas in our own culture in which we are called to obey God rather than men?

As with Daniel, how can we make sure God receives the glory for who He is and what He has done for us?

✋ Hands

What was it about Daniel's faith that made him a model servant? How does your faith impact the things you are involved in (school, sports, family life, etc.)?

How does Daniel's faithfulness challenge you to live out your own faith in the presence of others?

⭐ **The point: We worship God alone, and nothing else.**

▶ Read Daniel 3:8-12.

Pay close attention to verse 12 and note what the king demanded and how the Jews' (Shadrach, Meshach, and Abednego) responded.

Demand   Response

In chapter 2, King Nebuchadnezzar praised God after Daniel interpreted his dream correctly. When it benefited the king, he praised the God of the Jews. But when it didn't benefit him, the king lashed out in anger and sought to kill all those who opposed him and his laws. What do you think his behavior reveals about sinful human nature?

Knowing that this act was to show loyalty to the king, why do you think it was such a big deal for Shadrach, Meshach, and Abednego to refuse to bow down to the statue?

▶ Respond

Have you ever been persecuted or accused by someone because of your faith? How did you respond?

What are some ways you can make sure to worship God alone, despite persecution? (For example, you may want to have some close friends hold you accountable.) Record your response.

Commit to worship God alone, and ask Him to help you stand strong when those around you tempt you to worship other things.

⭐ The point: We can trust that God is sovereign and good.

▶ Read Daniel 3:13-23.

When King Nebuchadnezzar heard that the Jews refused to bow to his statue, he summoned them in a fit of rage. There he gave them a second chance to bow. Why do you think he did this rather than immediately sentencing them to death?

Reread verses 16-18. Even when the powerful king angrily promised them a painful death, the men still held tight to their faith. The king challenged their faith and demanded to know who would stand up to his own power to save them from the fiery furnace. In your own words, how did Shadrach, Meshach, Abednego respond?

In Romans 9:19-23, we see that God does not need to answer to man to justify His actions. This is the promise that we have when others challenge our faith: God does not bow to the demands of man. What does this reveal about God's character? How does this affect you personally?

▶ Respond

Doubting the sovereignty and goodness of God is easy when we allow ourselves to get caught up in our busy lives. Ask God to reveal areas of your life where you need His power to rescue you, and ask Him to grow in you a strong faith.

Nebuchadnezzar misunderstood who God was when he assumed God's power could not outweigh his own. Describe a time when you've seen someone go against God intentionally.

⭐ **The point: We can trust in God for protection.**

▶ Read Daniel 3:24-30.

How many men did Nebuchadnezzar throw into the fire? How many did he see?

What phrase did Nebuchadnezzar use to describe the fourth person in the fire? Why is this significant?

What was the king's response when he noticed the three men were unharmed? What do you think he had expected to happen to them?

Highlight the phrase: "not a hair of their heads was singed" (v. 27). Then, read Luke 12:7, and note again the attention drawn to the fact that God knows and cares about all the minute details of our lives—including how many hairs we have on our heads. In your own words, write what this reveals about the character of our Father.

▶ Respond

Often the best thing we can do when we feel alone and abandoned by people or by God is to recognize our daily blessings and acknowledge them.

Take some time right now to record ten blessings in your own life, even if they are as simple as having warm food to eat. Remember that some people don't even have the small things we take for granted—so thank God today for His provision and His protection.

Think of a recent circumstance during which you know God protected you. Describe that experience.

⭐ The point: Those who trust God are dedicated to Him in prayer.

Daniel's commitment to prayer and maintaining his relationship with God extended into every aspect of his life. Even when prayer was forbidden, Daniel's trust in and commitment to God remained strong.

▶ Read Daniel 6:1-10.

Daniel was an _____. The 120 _____ reported to him (vv. 1-2).

Why did the other administrators and satraps try to find a charge against Daniel?

What did the men believe they would find against Daniel? How did Daniel respond to their decree?

What strikes you about Daniel's response? Why?

▶ Respond

Set aside a certain amount of time this week to dedicate to prayer. Jot down your commitment and ask someone you trust to keep you accountable.

How do you need to adjust your time and priorities in order to make more time for prayer? Consider keeping a prayer journal.

★ ## The point: We can trust God and depend on Him for rescue.

▶ **Read Daniel 6:11-18.**

What did the men see when they found Daniel? How was this similar to or different from the way they would have found him any other day?

In what ways did Daniel demonstrate his dependence on God?

Was the king able to reverse the law? Why or why not?

What did the king tell Daniel as the men threw him into the lions' den (v. 16)?

How did this time of adversity reveal Daniel's character?

▶ **Respond**

Spend some time this week noting areas of your life where you find yourself struggling to trust God. Commit those parts of your life to Him, and ask Him to help you trust Him more.

Thank God that you can depend on Him in all things. Spend some time in prayer praising God that He is fully reliable and fully trustworthy.

GOD'S PROMISED RESTORATION

GOD'S PEOPLE MUST PRIORITIZE GOD'S WORD.

INTRODUCTION

Daniel lived as an exile in a foreign land, but he remained committed to his faith even in the midst of opposition. He refused to compromise on the commands of His God, and God was faithful not only to deliver him from danger but also to use his faithfulness to advance His kingdom. The story of Daniel helps us, as strangers and aliens in the world, to see how to live in the world without adopting the values and priorities of the world.

God is faithful to His Word. He was faithful to bring judgment on His people for their idolatry, and He would then be faithful to bring them out of exile and back to the land of their fathers. But as they returned, their celebration would be mixed with sadness at the state of their homeland. As the people of God began to return home, the question remained as to how they would reclaim their identity as God's chosen people.

 Can you share an example of restoration in your life, an occasion in which God has brought you back from difficulty or hardship?

SETTING THE CONTEXT

The Babylonians were conquered by the Persians. This new kingdom wanted its subjects to retain a sense of their own identity. To that end, Cyrus, the king, allowed the captives to return to their homeland and even rebuild the temple. So the Israelites made their journeys home to the promised land. Just as the Lord used the Babylonians to judge His people, He used Cyrus to begin their restoration. "The Return of Jewish Exiles to Judah" (p. 70) shows the paths the returning exiles took.

Among those who returned were Ezra the priest and Nehemiah. Ezra emphasized the need to return to the law of the Lord while Nehemiah orchestrated the rebuilding of the walls of protection around Jerusalem. In both cases, the sovereign hand of God not only allowed the exiles to return but also supplied the resources needed to rebuild the temple and the walls. God was restoring His people.

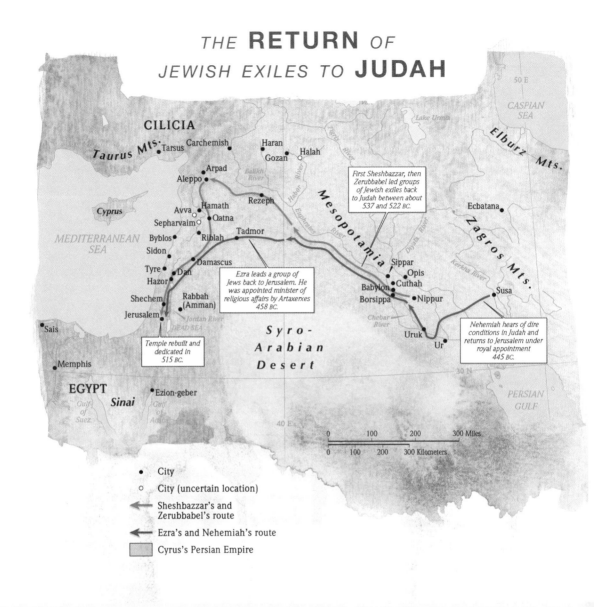

THE **RETURN** OF JEWISH EXILES TO **JUDAH**

First Sheshbazzar, then Zerubbabel led groups of Jewish exiles back to Judah between about 537 and 522 BC.

Ezra leads a group of Jews back to Jerusalem. He was appointed minister of religious affairs by Artaxerxes 458 BC.

Nehemiah hears of dire conditions in Judah and returns to Jerusalem under royal appointment 445 BC.

Temple rebuilt and dedicated in 515 BC.

- • City
- ○ City (uncertain location)
- ← Sheshbazzar's and Zerubbabel's route
- ← Ezra's and Nehemiah's route
- Cyrus's Persian Empire

SESSION VIDEOS

Watch this session's video, and then continue the group discussion using the following guide.

▶ What ideas or phrases stood out to you most in the video? Why?

▶ What were some of the specific challenges the exiles would have faced upon returning to their land?

GROUP DISCUSSION

As a group, read Ezra 3:8-13; 5:1-2.

⭐ Why would the reconstruction of the temple be such an important step in the people's return? What would it have meant to them?

▶ Why was there a mixed reaction to the laying of the foundation of the new temple?

▶ How have you experienced restoration bringing both joy and sadness at the same time?

The temple was the center of religious and spiritual life for Israel. The rebuilding of the temple and the altar in it was a priority for the people to reestablish their worship. In devoting themselves to rebuilding the temple, the people were demonstrating their desire for repentance of their idolatry, which had led to their exile.

It would be easy to think that those who wept were doing so for nostalgic reasons—they remembered the original temple in all its glory and were sad that it no longer stood. However, the way the passage reads indicates another way of looking at these tears—tears of gladness. Yes, there may be some sadness in their hearts because of their affiliation with the first temple. But the tears they cried when they saw the new foundation were tears of joy; in light of everything that had happened to them, God was faithful during all of the years in exile. He kept His promise to bring them back home. And they stood at the site of the new temple foundation, seeing with their own eyes the real and tangible grace of God in their lives.

As a group, read Nehemiah 2:17-18; 6:15-16.

▶ What are some logistical reasons why the rebuilding of the walls of Jerusalem was so significant?

★ What are some spiritual reasons? How would the rebuilding of the walls contribute to the spiritual lives of the Israelites?

The walls of Jerusalem, which provided protection from the surrounding nations, had been broken down and the gates had been burned. For Nehemiah, this was an unacceptable state. Restoring the walls would be a powerful symbol of God's restoration because the physical state of the city mirrored the spiritual and emotional state of its inhabitants. Nehemiah and the people persevered by faith through opposition, and the walls were rebuilt. God's strength and protection of His people were once again on display.

As a group, read Nehemiah 8:1-6.

★ How did the Jews respond to the reading of the law?

▶ Why do you think they were willing to listen to the reading of the law for several hours?

Throughout Israel's history, idolatry was at the root of their rebellion against God. Because of their sin, God's people spent over 70 years in exile. Once they moved back to Jerusalem, they were able to gather publicly and worship the Lord by listening to His Word. The event was timely, because the Law required the nation to gather to hear the Word of God read every seven years (Deut. 31:9-13).

► How can you tell if a church is centered on the proclamation of God's Word or on something else? Why is gathering to hear God's Word so important for believers?

The Israelites' response was probably an amazing sight. First, all the people stood when Ezra opened up the Scriptures. Ezra opened in prayer and declared praise to God, causing the people to raise their hands and proclaim, "Amen, Amen." Not only that, but they listened to God's Word together. True biblical revival is experienced in community. In addition to confessing our sins to God, the next step is confessing our sins to one another in order to extend forgiveness to others in the same way we've been forgiven by God. Then and only then will we experience the joy of revival in community!

CHRIST CONNECTION

God brought the exiles back to the land, and faithful leaders rebuilt the temple for worship and the city walls for protection, but this would not be permanent. Through Jesus' death and resurrection, He made a way for His people to be protected from the enemies of sin and death and to worship in Spirit and truth forever.

OUR MISSION

Head

God's promise of return was fulfilled under His sovereign direction after 70 years of exile. What does this say about the importance of waiting on the Lord and relying on His timing?

Why do we so often fail to crave God's Word as we should?

Heart

What are the dangers in thinking that worship is something that only takes place during a church service?

If worship is primarily of the heart, how has your worship been lately? Are you currently finding satisfaction and joy in God? If not, why do you think that is the case?

Hands

Why is it important for younger Christians to build relationships with older Christians? What are the dangers of never having older Christians who speak into your life?

When has someone helped you understand something in Scripture that was difficult to understand? When have you helped someone else understand something in Scripture?

⭐ **The point: God fulfilled His promise when He brought His people home.**

▶ Read Ezra 1:1-8.

Since the Israelites had been in captivity 70 years, most of them had only heard about Jerusalem. What do you think it was like for them to finally receive permission to return there?

What does the Israelites' return from exile tell you about God's character?

Although the Israelites suffered difficult circumstances, such as exile to Babylon, God did not leave them without hope. Even before their exile, He gave them encouraging promises, telling them what would happen and that He would deliver them. What promises in God's Word have been especially meaningful to you?

▶ Respond

Read Jeremiah 29:11 again. God gave His people this promise before they went into exile. He gave them encouragement that their nation wouldn't end with their captivity. He had a plan and a future for His chosen people.

Spend some time thanking God that He always keeps His promises. Share with Him any situations in which you're struggling to trust Him, and ask Him to give you faith to trust Him.

⭐ **The point: Before they began rebuilding, God's people gathered together in worship.**

▶ **Read Ezra 3:1-7.**

According to verse 2, what did the people build? Why?

What does this say about the importance of making worship a priority in our lives?

Highlight the phrase, "even though they feared the surrounding peoples" (v. 3). What other emotions or circumstances might keep people from worshiping God (being distracted, angry, etc.)?

Why is it important not to let our emotions or circumstances keep us from worshiping God?

List several reasons why God is worthy to be worshiped.

▶ **Respond**

The Israelites worshiped God with cheerful hearts before they even had a place to worship Him.

Think about your own worship. What are some obstacles that prevent you from worshiping God? What can you change to remove those obstacles, or how can you continue to worship in spite of them?

Jot down some of your favorite ways to worship God. Make a point to engage in one of those this week.

PERSONAL STUDY: DAY 3

⭐ **The point: God's people proclaimed His goodness.**

▶ Read Ezra 3:8-13.

The Israelites gathered to celebrate the laying of the temple's foundation, but what was the primary purpose of their gathering?

What were some of the ways the Israelites engaged in worship?

What are some of the ways believers today worship God?

List some similarities and differences between the Israelites' worship and our worship today.

Israelites' Worship   Our Worship

▶ Respond

Do you ever worship in unique ways, other than singing? Shouting? Painting? Praying the Psalms aloud? Take a few minutes and worship God. Sing, if you want, but feel free to express your adoration to Him in other ways as well, such as playing an instrument, writing a poem of praise, and so on. Praise Him for His faithfulness to you.

Text or call a friend and tell him or her at least one way God has shown His goodness to you this week.

⭐ **The point: God's people should pray while taking action.**

▶ **Read Nehemiah 2:1-8.**

What did Nehemiah do while he answered the king?

What can we learn about prayer from Nehemiah in this passage?

List Nehemiah's requests to the king.

What was the king's response?

▶ **Read Luke 11:9.**

What three things did Jesus instruct people to "keep" doing?

Summarize Jesus' promised results if people keep doing these things.

▶ **Respond**

Think about your own life. When have you prayed about something while still working toward a solution? In what ways did God answer those prayers?

⭐ **The point: God's enemies will attempt to discourage His people, but His people will prevail.**

▶ Read Nehemiah 6:1-14.

Circle the number of times Sanballat and his men tried to meet with Nehemiah. What does this say about their desire to stop the work?

Sanballat's tactic shifted to attacks on Nehemiah's character. How did Nehemiah respond?

In what way did Sanballat use those inside the Jewish community to try and end the project? How did Nehemiah expose this plan?

How does Satan use similar tactics in an attempt to hinder God's work today?

What did Nehemiah do instead of seeking revenge?

Jot down a few words to describe Nehemiah's character and faith in God.

▶ Respond

List some ways the enemy tries to discourage you. Ask God to strengthen you and help you stand firm.

Have you ever unfairly attacked someone's character? Confess this to the Lord and ask Him to forgive you. If necessary, make steps toward reconciliation.

GOD'S ETERNAL PLAN

WORSHIP INVOLVES GIVING GOD OUR VERY BEST.

INTRODUCTION

Just as the prophets foretold, the same God who brought judgment on His people through foreign rulers worked in the hearts of foreign rulers to allow them to come back to their homeland. Once they returned to Israel, their leaders led them to rebuild the temple and the walls around Jerusalem and to recommit themselves to the law of God they had abandoned over the years.

While the people were aware of their sin that had led them into captivity, they would still be unable to keep the law they had committed themselves to. They were still living with old hearts, and they needed the new hearts promised in the new covenant. As time went on, the people indeed kept themselves from the idolatry of their past, but their hearts strayed from God in a different way. Shallow worship revealed that although they might have achieved a measure of external obedience, their hearts were still far from God.

 Why is it often easier to focus our attention on external behavior rather than the sin issue of the heart?

SETTING THE CONTEXT

Sadly, within a few decades of the rebuilding of the temple, the prophet Malachi had to deliver his message because the worship of the people had grown stale. He focused on the failure of the priests to fear God and to serve the people conscientiously during difficult times, but the priests mirrored the people—they all lacked the sincere worship God commanded.

The Book of Malachi is the last prophetic message from God before the close of the Old Testament. Then came four hundred years of silence from God. Malachi, like many prophets before him, gave the people a severe warning, but he also spoke of the hope to come. As "Seeing Jesus in the Return from Exile" (p. 82) shows, the Messiah was coming, and He was coming to deal with the true problem of humanity—the sin in our hearts. But would the people be ready for Him?

SEEING *JESUS* IN THE
RETURN *FROM* EXILE

	OLD TESTAMENT	NEW TESTAMENT

OLD TESTAMENT	NEW TESTAMENT
Cyrus the Persian Anointed by God to Rule and Rebuild the Temple (Isa. 44:24–45:7)	**Jesus the Messiah** Anointed by God to Rule— He Is the Temple (John 1:41; 2:21)
Zerubbabel A Descendant of Jehoiachin; Returned from the Exile (1 Chron. 3:17-19)	**Jesus Christ** A Descendant of Zerubbabel; the End of the Exile (Matt. 1:12-17)
Ezra Devoted Himself to Studying, Obeying, and Teaching the Law of the Lord (Ezra 7:10)	**Jesus** The Scriptures, Including the Law of the Lord, Testify About Him (John 5:39,46)
Nehemiah A Man of Prayer (Neh. 1:5-11; 2:4; 4:9; 5:19; 6:9,14; 13:14,22,29,31)	**Jesus** A Man of Prayer (Matt. 26:36-44; Luke 11:1-13; John 17; Rom. 8:34; Heb. 7:25)
The Sun of Righteousness Will Rise with Healing in Its Wings (Mal. 4:2)	**The Dawn** Jesus Will Visit Us and Guide Us into the Way of Peace (Luke 1:78-79)

SESSION VIDEOS

Watch this session's video, and then continue the group
discussion using the following guide.

▶ What ideas or phrases stood out to you most in the video? Why?

▶ What does the people's return to vain worship after returning to the
promised land teach us about sinful human nature?

GROUP DISCUSSION

As a group, read Malachi 1:6-10.

▶ What were some of the failures of the priests mentioned in this passage?

★ How do those failures relate to the heart behind the act of worship?

▶ Why are failures like these so offensive to the Lord?

Notice that God gave two indictments against His people at the beginning: they showed Him no honor, and they showed Him no fear. Not only did they not honor and fear Him, but they despised His name.

Despising means having an attitude of ongoing disrespect for someone or something; it refers to the act of conveying insignificance or worthlessness upon an object, idea, or individual. The text shows us that the people did this to God by offering crippled, lame, or blinded animals to the Lord rather than the perfect, blameless sacrifice He requested. He even asked them, "Do you think that if you gave even the governor what you're giving me that he'd be okay with it?"

▶ In what ways do people "despise" God's name today? How can you guard against this in your own life?

As a group, read Malachi 3:7-12.

▶ In what sense were the people robbing God?

★ Why do you think God cares so much about our finances? What do our finances reveal about our hearts?

After hearing from God, the Israelites questioned their departure from God by denying that they ever left in the first place. After all, they still sacrificed to Him, right?

Before we harshly judge the Israelites, we must remember how easy it is to wander. "Far from God?" a churchgoer might say. "I am not far from God! I go to church every week! How can you say that I am far from God?" Many are blinded to the fact that they are blind.

Essentially, God told the Israelites that despite their protestations, they were far from Him. God had challenged the Israelites previously for their poor sacrifices, their lack of worship, their idolatry, and their faithlessness. The root of the problem is the heart. They had misappropriated their funds. In other words, they failed to deal responsibly with what God had given them. Giving is an indication of the state of our hearts and measures how much we value God.

As a group, read Malachi 4:1-6.

★ Why is it fitting that the entire Old Testament closes with the threat of a curse?

▶ Despite the curse, where do you see the shadow of the gospel in these verses?

The text speaks of a future light in the midst of Israel's darkness. Israel expected unending blessings because of their position as God's chosen people. However, God first informed them that He would come to set all wrongs right—beginning the process with their lukewarm worship.

The final two verses of Malachi offer the ultimate cliffhanger of the Old Testament. He ends with a promise of someone to come and a warning about things already done. "Look," Malachi wrote, "I am going to send you Elijah the prophet before Day of the Lord comes. He will turn the hearts of fathers to their children and the hearts of children to their fathers. Otherwise, I will come and strike the land with a curse."

CHRIST CONNECTION

After Malachi, the prophetic word of God went silent for four hundred years. But Malachi prophesied about a messenger who would prepare the way for the Messiah to bring God's kingdom. Centuries later, John the Baptist arrived as the messenger who prepared the way for Jesus. The last word of the Old Testament is "curse," a reminder of the consequence of our sin. But in the New Testament, one of the first words we hear from Jesus is "blessing." The One who bears our curse is the One who brings us blessing.

OUR MISSION

◐ Head

Sometimes people assume they are in a right relationship with God, but they are not. What are some ways we can guard against having such a false notion?

What are some areas of life where students struggle to give God their best?

♥ Heart

How does this passage relate to Jesus' words about our hearts being where our treasure is?

What do we communicate about our view of God and His grace toward us when we fail to give Him our very best?

Hands

What are some ways you are intentionally seeking to be a blessing to others with your time, talents, and treasures?

How might your blessing others in this way point them to Christ?

✪ The point: Shallow worship shows disregard for God's greatness.

▶ Read Malachi 1:6-14.

According to verse 6, what two attributes did the Israelites fail to possess in their acts of worship? What else did they do that dishonored God?

Why were these such serious offenses?

God stated that He would rather see the temple closed completely than see it defiled with insincere worship. Their careless actions regarding worship revealed the condition of their hearts. List some of the sinful ways the Israelites handled their offerings.

Because the Israelites neglected the necessary fear and honor for the Lord, they began to see worship as a burden rather than a privilege. How does a healthy fear of God help you honor Him in your worship?

How might a careless attitude toward worship reveal a problem with your view of God?

▶ Respond

Think about your own life. Ask the Holy Spirit to guide you as you examine your heart. Ask yourself: What is my attitude toward God's greatness? How is that revealed in my actions?

Spend a moment in prayer asking God to remind you of His greatness in a way that will be reflected in your worship.

⭐ **The point: True worship reveres the name of God and recognizes that He is great.**

▶ **Read Psalm 96:1-6.**

This Psalm is not just about a feeling toward God; it is about action. Look back at these verses and underline the action words: (sing, praise, proclaim, and declare.) What do these words tell you about the way you should respond to God?

Worship isn't just an idea—it is a way of life that actively and specifically acknowledges the presence of God. Fill in the blanks according to the Psalmist's instructions:

Sing a _____ _____

Praise His _____

Proclaim His _____

Declare His _____

What reasons did the psalmist give for praising the Lord?

▶ **Respond**

The psalmist specifically referred to God by the name Yahweh and praised His salvation and His creation. What other attributes or names of God come to mind when you think about His greatness? List a few here.

How has God been at work in your life? Looking at the list of names or characteristics you just made. In what specific ways has God revealed Himself to you?

What is one specific way you can declare this great attribute of God to those you encounter this week?

⭐ **The point: Shallow worship minimizes God's worth.**

▶ Read Malachi 3:7-12.

How were the Israelites robbing God?

If the Israelites would return to God, what did He promise to do for them?

What did God tell the Israelites to do that may have seemed radical to them (v. 10)?

Why do you think it often seems radical to obey God in even the simplest ways?

Testing God out of rebellion is sinful, but testing His faithfulness through obedience can be an act of worship. Returning to God means that we acknowledge His control and authority over all that we have. Giving becomes easy when we keep this perspective.

▶ Respond

Have you ever felt like you were going through the motions of Christianity without really being in fellowship with God? This is shallow worship. What are some specific ways you can be more present in your fellowship with God?

List two ways you can return to God through obedience this week.

✪ The point: True worship recognizes God's stature, power, and holiness.

▶ **Read Psalm 96:7-9.**

The Psalmist repeated the phrase "ascribe to the Lord." Look at the definition of the word *ascribe*. According to these verses, what characteristics belong to God?

If you recognize God for who He truly is and give Him the glory and honor due to His name, then how should we view God? How can we truly praise Him?

▶ **Read Malachi 3:13-18.**

Our worship gets off track when we begin to focus on other people, our things, or ourselves more than we focus on God. The Israelites were comparing themselves to outsiders rather than focusing on God's goodness. From their viewpoint, what was unfair about following God?

When God corrected their thinking (vv. 16-18), what outcome did He promise?

What are some ways you hear people speak out against God in today's culture? Give some examples.

▶ **Respond**

What would it look like to you to worship the Lord in the splendor of His holiness? How does your view of yourself change when you focus on God's glory and strength?

Write out your own prayer of praise to God, modeled after Psalm 96:7-9. Praise Him in these ways each day this week.

⭐ **The point: Genuine worship is empowered by the Holy Spirit.**

▶ **Read John 4:23-24.**

Jesus responded here to a woman who was attempting to distract Him with a legalistic question about worship practices of her day. He referenced "true worshipers." Does this imply that there can be "false worshipers"? Explain the difference.

What does it mean to worship in spirit and truth? Can you worship in spirit but not truth? Or in truth but not in spirit? Explain.

What significant reason was given for our need to worship in spirit?

▶ **Respond**

Remembering that God is Spirit reminds us that He is greater than all we see and experience here on earth. Only through the power of the Holy Spirit can we engage in genuine worship.

In what way do you rely on the Spirit in your worship? Give some examples.

How can you practice repentance in your efforts to worship in truth? What would that look like for you this week?

For further study on the Holy Spirit, read John 14:26 and Luke 3:16.

HOW TO USE THE LEADER GUIDE

Prepare to Lead

The Leader Guide is designed to be cut out along the dotted line so you, the leader, can have this front-and-back page with you as you lead your group through the session.

Watch the session video and *read through the session content* with the Leader Guide cut-out in hand and notice how it supplements each section of the study.

Use the *Session Objective* in the Leader Guide to help focus your preparation and leadership in the group session.

Questions & Answers

⭐ Questions in the session content with this icon have some sample answers provided in the Leader Guide, if needed, to help you jump-start or steer the conversation.

Setting the Context

This section of the session always has an *infographic* on the opposite page. The Leader Guide provides an activity to help your group members interact with the content communicated through the infographic.

Group Discussion

The Group Discussion contains the main teaching content for each session, providing questions for students to interact with as you move through the biblical passages. Some of these questions will have suggested answers in the Leader Guide.

Our Mission ⭕ ⓥ ✋

The Our Mission is a summary application section designed to highlight how the biblical passages being studied challenge the way we think, feel, and live today. Some of these questions will have suggested answers in the Leader Guide.

Pray

Conclude each group session with a prayer. A brief sample prayer is provided at the end of each Leader Guide cut-out.

Session Objective

Show that even though God's people have failed to love and obey Him repeatedly, God continues to pursue them, extend His faithful love to them, and advance His plan to purchase them from sin through Jesus.

Introducing the Study

Use this intro to discuss the importance of how messages are communicated as a way to set up the story of Hosea.

Setting the Context

Use the following activity to help group members see the good news of the prophets.

Point out Hosea's connection to Jesus on "Seeing Jesus in the Prophets" (p. 10) and say that this prophet's message is the one we will be studying in this session. Then ask the following questions: "Why are the prophetic books some of the most overlooked books in Scripture?" "How can seeing the prophets' connections to the gospel and Jesus help to unlock the messages of these prophets for us?"

Read this paragraph to transition to the next part of the study:

The messages of the prophets may be difficult in the details, but they are simple in their intent: God wanted His people to repent of sin, be warned of coming judgment, hear again about His love, and live in light of hope. With this framework, it isn't hard to see how the prophets help to set up the coming of Jesus for the salvation of sinners.

Group Discussion

Watch this session's video, and then as part of the group discussion, use these answers as needed for the questions highlighted in this section.

⭐ How are we like Gomer in our relationship with God, and God like Hosea? *1) God has bound Himself to us as His people, even though we often act unfaithfully. 2) We can prostitute ourselves with idols and gods of our own making. 3) We repeatedly show our unfaithfulness to the God who has loved us and always been faithful to us.*

⭐ What does this passage teach us about the nature of true love? *1) True love seeks purity in the person and in the relationship. 2) True love is forgiving and forever. 3) True love brings peace and security.*

⭐ How does this remind us of what God has done for us in the gospel? *1) Though we rightfully belong to God as His created image bearers, He paid the ransom for our sin to free us and bring us home with Him once again. 2) Though we have turned away from God again and again, He continues to welcome us home when we repent and return to Him once more. 3) The gospel makes us right with God by faith, but it also entails our sanctification, our eventual purity, by the work of the Holy Spirit.*

Our Mission

♥ How do we, based on our usage of the word in our culture, define love? How is that different than the picture of God's love we see in Scripture? *This picture of the love of God stands in stark contrast to what passes for love in our culture. We love sports, movies, pets, food, actors, games, and a host of other things. We throw around the word without thinking about it; it's part of our regular vocabulary. It seems that to us, at least based on the way we use the word, love is a feeling or emotion. According to that mind-set, love is not commitment based but sits on the shaky foundation of personal preference and taste. In God, we find the true definition of the word love. It's a definition forged not with word, but with action, exemplified by the work of Jesus on the cross.*

✋ Why do you think God asked Hosea to marry this woman? Why was it not sufficient for Hosea to deliver God's message with words alone? *Having been pursued and loved by God, and in light of the great personal cost to Himself, we are called to extend that same pursuit and love to others. We love because we have been loved (1 John 4:11). As in the case of Hosea, this love for others is not emotional attachment, and it's not without cost. To pursue others with the message of the gospel will be a costly endeavor—it will cost us time and the realignment of priorities. But when the cost might seem to be too great, it's helpful for us to call to mind the great cost that God Himself paid for us.*

Pray

Close your group in prayer, praising God that He does not leave us in our disobedience but instead has paid the price for us to return to Him in purity.

SESSION 2 • LEADER GUIDE

Session Objective

Show that God's love and compassion were not just for the people of Israel but for the entire world, and use Jonah as a foreshadowing of how the people would lose sight of this and wrongly believe salvation was only for themselves.

Introducing the Study

Use this intro to highlight that the main character and hero in the book of Jonah isn't Jonah himself but God.

Setting the Context

Use the following activity to help group members see God's compassion toward the nations.

Call attention to "God's Compassion Toward the Nations" (p. 22). Ask group members to comment on the variety of people in this list who receive God's compassion (a prostitute and a Gentile army commander; both men and women; individuals and an entire city). Then ask the following questions: "What does this list say about our reservations regarding certain people, people groups, or nations receiving God's compassion?" "How have we already received the good news of God's compassion for the nations?"

Read this paragraph to transition to the next part of the study:

God's compassion toward the nations has been extended toward us in the gospel of Jesus, the availability of God's Word, and the loving fellowship of the church. Let us receive this compassion with gratitude and share it joyfully with all others.

Group Discussion

Watch this session's video, and then as part of the group discussion, use these answers as needed for the questions highlighted in this section.

⭐ What are some reasons we might run from the call of God? *1) Fear of the consequences, whether emotional, social, financial, or physical. 2) We don't agree with God's decision. 3) Obedience might upset too much the stability of our lives.*

★ What can we learn about evangelism from what happened in Nineveh? *1) God can reach people who would seem hardened and antagonistic toward Him. 2) God works through His people in order to draw the nations to Himself. 3) Even a message of judgment from the Lord can humble a heart.*

★ How should our prayers both for ourselves and others change in light of these passages from Jonah? *1) We should pray for hearts that reflect God's concern for the nations. 2) We should pray for forgiveness for our prejudice and bias, as these are sinful in the eyes of God. 3) We should pray for the nations to hear the gospel of Jesus Christ and believe God's Word for their own salvation.*

Our Mission

♥ What did God want Jonah to realize with His question about Jonah's anger (Jonah 4:4)? *In essence, God used this to prompt Jonah to examine the racial bias in his heart. God was not merely the God of the Israelites, but the God and Savior of the entire world. Like Jonah, we must confront the long-held prejudice and hatred in our hearts that might cause us to withhold forgiveness and compassion from others. When we bear ill will toward others, we show that we have not truly understood and experienced the fullness of God's grace given to us.*

✋ Does it surprise you that Jonah's simple message was so effective? Why or why not? *When we are called to speak the Word of God, we might feel inadequate, afraid, or vulnerable as we do it. But the bowing of the mighty city of Nineveh reminds us that God's Word is living, active, and able to cut through to the soul and spirit of mankind. We can speak the Word of God confidently, not because we are great orators, but because of the inherent power present in the gospel message of Jesus Christ.*

Pray

Close your group in prayer, asking God to help you see the rest of the world with the same eyes of compassion that He has.

SESSION 3 · LEADER GUIDE

Session Objective

Show that the people's rebellion culminated in open idolatry for which both nations were judged and taken into captivity. This marks a low point for God's people—out of the land again but this time because of their sin. This session should convey the heaviness of God's judgment. In conclusion, hint at the hope that remains—the remnant of Israel would one day be restored, which leads to the final Old Testament sessions.

Introducing the Study

Use this intro to discuss God's continued pursuit of Israel even through their disobedience.

Setting the Context

Use the following activity to help group members see the need for God's King to come.

Point group members to "Kings of the Divided Kingdom" (p. 34). Allow them a moment to share any initial observations of the content on this page (David is the benchmark for evaluating the kings; so few kings who did what was right; so many kings who did what was evil; the descendants of David in Judah were scattered). Explain that Israel experienced several different dynasties of various lengths, but Judah's kings were all descendants of David. Then ask the following questions: "Does seeing the kings of Israel and Judah in this context surprise you? Why or why not?" "What does this evaluation of the kings and the resulting judgment on the nations teach us about leadership?" "What are your thoughts on the line of kings through Judah's history serving as the family tree for Jesus?"

Group Discussion

Watch this session's video, and then as part of the group discussion, use these answers as needed for the questions highlighted in this section.

⭐ What can you learn about the character of God from these verses? *1) God is faithful to His word, both for blessing and for judgment. 2) God despises idolatry and disobedience. 3) God is patient and compassionate, pleading with people to turn from their wicked ways.*

⭐ Why is pride so destructive in the lives of God's people? *1) Pride leads us to think we can do things on our own and do them better than God. 2) Pride in our hearts puts ourselves on the throne above God so that we glorify ourselves instead of Him. 3) Pride takes our eyes off our mission to proclaim the good news of Jesus in the world.*

⭐ Where do you see hope in these verses, even in the midst of judgment? *1) There were people who survived the judgment of God, albeit in the form of exile and servitude. 2) There was fulfillment of God's word, which gave hope that His promises to Abraham and David could still be fulfilled. 3) God promised an end to the exile after seventy years through the prophet Jeremiah.*

Our Mission

⭕ Why do you think pride comes along with hardness of heart? *Lack of repentance walks hand in hand with pride. Zedekiah had every opportunity to repent or return to the Lord. He could have listened to the council of Jeremiah, humbly acknowledged the Word of the Lord, and demonstrated that acknowledgment by turning away from his own wisdom and coming back to the Lord. However, Zedekiah was convinced his way was right, and he felt no need to turn away from it.*

✋ Why do you think God desires His people to be distinct and set apart from the world in the way that they live? *Another sign of hardness of heart in these verses is the lack of distinction between God's people and the rest of the nations. From the beginning, God planned for the people of Israel be a people of distinction on the earth. They alone would shine forth His glory as a kingdom of priests set apart specifically for the Lord. But in the days of Zedekiah, "all the leaders of the priests and the people multiplied their unfaithful deeds, imitating all the detestable practices of the nations" (2 Chron. 36:14a). In other words, they abandoned their distinction as God's people and began to follow the ways of everyone around them instead.*

Pray

Close your group in prayer, asking God to give you courage to confront your own pride and idolatry and to call others to do the same.

SESSION 4 · LEADER GUIDE

Session Objective

Show that even in Israel's darkest hour, God continued to shower them with hope, hope that God was going to provide them with a Suffering Servant who would pay for their sins and who would initiate a new covenant—one where God's law was put on their hearts.

Introducing the Study

Use this intro to discuss the importance of Isaiah 53 when it comes to Old Testament prophecy.

Setting the Context

Use the following activity to help group members see the biblical significance of the new covenant.

Ask group members to look over "The New Covenant" (p. 46) and to consider what a "permanent covenant" means. Furthermore, ask group members to discuss why the Mosaic covenant is not considered a "permanent covenant." Explain that a "permanent covenant" means God Himself will accomplish the fulfillment of this covenant and its implications will last for all eternity. The Mosaic covenant is unique in this list for its promise of a curse for disobedience.

Read this paragraph to transition to the next part of the study:

Each of these covenants points to Jesus Christ as its fulfillment: Jesus is the blessing and offspring of Abraham; Jesus is the Son of David on the eternal throne; and Jesus is the sacrifice that inaugurates the new covenant. And Jesus perfectly obeys the commands of the Mosaic covenant while simultaneously taking upon Himself the curse for our disobedience. This is the hope the whole world needs to hear.

Group Discussion

Watch this session's video, and then as part of the group discussion, use these answers as needed for the questions highlighted in this section.

⭐ What are some of the ways you see the life and death of Jesus foreshadowed in this prophecy? *1) Jesus was pierced for our rebellion (v. 5). 2) Jesus was silent before His accusers (v. 7). 3) Jesus was crucified as a criminal and buried in the borrowed tomb of Joseph of Arimathea, a rich man (v. 9).*

⭐ Why might this prophecy have been so encouraging to God's people when they were in exile? *1) It showed that God still claimed His people as His own. 2) It spoke of God's comfort for His people in bringing them back to their land. 3) The prophecy promised to turn their mourning into joy as God provided for all their needs.*

⭐ Where do you see the gospel in this prophecy? *1) God will change the hearts of His people with His teachings. 2) This new covenant will be accomplished completely by God. 3) The new covenant will deal fully and finally with the problem of sin.*

Our Mission

🅥 Worldly wisdom will tell people "trust your heart" or "believe in yourself." How do the passages in this session challenge this way of thinking? *This new covenant isn't written on tablets or paper, but in our hearts. Paul commented on this reality in 2 Corinthians 5. In verse 17, he wrote, "If anyone is in Christ, he is a new creation; old things have passed away, and look, new things have come." When we believe the message of the gospel, the old self dies, and we are spiritually resurrected with Christ. Our new self, with a new heart, has new desires, new tastes, and most importantly, a new Master. No longer are we imprisoned by sin; instead, God indwells our hearts through the presence of the Holy Spirit.*

✋ How has this session encouraged and challenged you when it comes to your own relationship to God? *Knowing God is a two-sided coin. The first side of the coin is our personal relationship with God—a return to intimacy with God as seen in the garden. The other side of the coin is the desire to make God known. This is also part of our return to God's original intent for humanity. Adam and Eve not only knew God, they were also given the job of reflecting God and making much of Him in everything they did. Like them, we are called to spread the glory of God throughout the earth, making the gospel of Jesus known to everyone around us.*

Pray

Close your group in prayer, thanking God for the sure and certain hope that we have in the gospel.

SESSION 5 · LEADER GUIDE

Session Objective

Show that following God can sometimes come at great cost and that God is to be glorified and His kingdom advanced no matter what the cost. God gives the strength to follow Him and to endure any hardship that might come our way because of our faithfulness to Him.

Introducing the Study

Use this intro to set up Daniel's story of faithfulness to God during persecution.

Setting the Context

Use the following activity to help group members see how God's wisdom through His people blesses the world, even when faithfulness leads to suffering.

Direct your group to look over "Daniel's Life" (p. 58) and to call out the familiar stories they see. Then ask the following questions:

• Why should the wisdom of God be considered valuable among God's people and for unbelievers? *God's wisdom explains how the world should operate, and it provides supernatural information and direction for the blessing of the world. In other words, God's wisdom from God's people helps fulfill His promise of blessing to the nations.*

• What should we make of the dangers faced by these exiles because of their faithfulness to God? *Living for the glory of God in a world that seeks its own glory will put Christians at odds with others, and this can lead to many painful consequences. But if the source of our faith is true—and He is—then standing for the name of Jesus, regardless of danger makes the most sense in the world.*

Group Discussion

Watch this session's video, and then as part of the group discussion, use these answers as needed for the questions highlighted in this section.

⭐ How would you describe Daniel? *1) Daniel was faithful to his God. 2) Daniel was persistent in his spiritual disciplines. 3) Daniel sought the favor of God above concern for his own life.*

101

⭐ What must Daniel have believed to be true about God to remain faithful? *1) That God's glory was more important than even his own life. 2) That God exists and rewards those who seek him (Heb. 11:6). 3) That God's will will be accomplished, regardless of how human beings plan and scheme.*

⭐ How does this proclamation reveal both God's mission and His glory? *1) God desires that His glory be known throughout the whole earth. 2) God's people saved from sin for all eternity will include those from every people, nation, and language on the earth—a kingdom greater than all those on earth. 3) God's people, miracles, and message all combine to show unbelievers that God alone is worthy of glory and He alone has the power to save.*

Our Mission

○ How does this account give you a different perspective on personal trials, allowing you to step back and see the bigger picture of God's work? *God chose to glorify Himself through miraculously saving Daniel in the lions' den. God used Daniel's trial and difficulties, however stressful they may have been to Daniel, to point unbelievers to Himself. As a result, a pagan king witnessed the miraculous hand of God and publicly proclaimed God's greatness. In fact, Darius went so far as to say that God's kingdom would have no end and that He is without rival. This should automatically lead us to wonder how God is using our own trials and sufferings to make much of Himself.*

✋ How does Daniel's faithfulness challenge you to live out your own faith in the presence of others? *Even though it would have been a good time for Daniel to take a month off from being faithful to God, he persevered. From a worldly standpoint, Daniel's faithfulness wasn't personally convenient; however, obedience to and love for God was deeply ingrained in Daniel. He did not shove his spiritual disciplines into the shadows of privacy. He had honored God in this manner the entire time He was in Babylon, and he would not stop now—not for a month, not even for a moment.*

Pray

Close your group in prayer, asking for the wisdom and courage to stand faithfully and rightly for the name of Jesus even in hostile circumstances.

SESSION 6 · LEADER GUIDE

Session Objective

Show that God brought His people out of exile and used various leaders to work together to rebuild the city to resume worship and prepare for the arrival of the Messiah.

Introducing the Study

Use this intro to set up the story of God's faithfulness in bringing His people out of exile.

Setting the Context

Use the following activity to help group members see the significance of God's work in "the second exodus."

Call attention to "The Return of Jewish Exiles to Judah" (p. 70). Explain that sometimes this event is called "the second exodus" because of references by the prophets (Isa. 11:10-16; Jer. 16:14-15; Mic. 7:14-20). Then ask the following questions: "What are similarities and differences between the first and second exodus?" "How might the return of the exiles compare to our lives as Christians?"

Read this paragraph to transition to the next part of the study:

The Lord used Cyrus to free His people to return home and worship Him. In fact, Isaiah 45 refers to Cyrus as the Lord's anointed. But though the people were being restored to the land, their restoration was incomplete. God had greater plans to accomplish, which included sending Jesus, His Anointed One, to save His people.

Group Discussion

Watch this session's video, and then as part of the group discussion, use these answers as needed for the questions highlighted in this section.

⭐ Why would the reconstruction of the temple be such an important step in the people's return? What would it have meant to them? *1) The reconstructed temple would have been a significant restoration of their worship of the one true God. 2) It would have been big step toward a return to normalcy. 3) It would have communicated to the people that God was present with them once more.*

★ What are some spiritual reasons? How would the rebuilding of the walls contribute to the spiritual lives of the Israelites? *1) The rebuilt walls would have comforted the people that God was with them once again. 2) The walls would have ensured the safety of their worship of the one true God. 3) The walls would give them faith that what God had torn down He had the power to rebuild.*

★ How did the Jews respond to the reading of the law? *1) The people listened attentively for six hours. 2) The people stood up in reverence for the reading of God's law. 3) The people bowed down and worshiped the Lord in response to His law.*

Our Mission

♥ What are the dangers in thinking that worship is something that only takes place during a church service? *As these chapters showed, neither experiencing the presence of God nor the opportunity to worship Him are attached to a geographical location. This reality is further emphasized in the New Testament as Christ followers are said to be the very temple of God by the indwelling of the Holy Spirit in them (1 Cor. 3:16-17; Eph. 4:30). Worship is first and foremost an issue of the heart—an internal joy and satisfaction in who God is and what He has done. Because of that, all of life is worship, offering us moments to take joy in God even in the smallest tasks of our day.*

✋ Why is it important for younger Christians to build relationships with older Christians? What are the dangers of never having older Christians who speak into your life? *We learn from these chapters that both young and old people lifted praises to God with various expressions and from different stages of life. Not only that, but those praises produced a unified sound that glorified the Lord and could be heard from far away. Thus, far from being an event designed for only one generation, we see all of God's people united in proclaiming the goodness of God to those around them. Such demonstration is a powerful witness to the world.*

Pray

Close your group in prayer, thanking God that our true protection comes not from physical walls but through the death and resurrection of Jesus.

SESSION 7 · LEADER GUIDE

Session Objective

Show that the stage was set for the arrival of the Messiah, but once again, God warned His people of their sin—now idolatry had been replaced with shallow worship. This session should be hopeful but also foreboding. The Messiah was coming, but would they be ready for Him? We see in the Gospels that they would not be.

Introducing the Study

Use this intro to introduce the context of shallow worship replacing idolatry in the lives of the Israelites.

Setting the Context

Use the following activity to help group members see how God used the people during the return from exile to foreshadow the coming of His Son, Jesus Christ.

Direct your group to review the connections on "Seeing Jesus in the Return from Exile" (p. 82). Ask them to identify the connection that seems most unlikely compared with the others (Cyrus the Persian) and to discuss its significance for our worldview. Then ask the following questions:

• How was God keeping His promises in these connections? *God promised to restore His people to the land after their exile; Zerubbabel is a continued fulfillment of God's promise to David that his descendant would have a forever throne.*

• What are some ways you see the gospel foreshadowed in this part of the biblical storyline? *The Davidic descendant is restored to Jerusalem, and his main concern is the right worship of the one true God; the law exposed the sin of the people upon their return and points forward to Jesus, the only One who can save from sin.*

Group Discussion

Watch this session's video, and then as part of the group discussion, use these answers as needed for the questions highlighted in this section.

⭐ How do those failures relate to the heart behind the act of worship? *1) Despising the Lord's name indicates a lack of fear and respect for the Creator God. 2) Presenting defiled and unworthy sacrifices on the Lord's altar showed they did not take the sin of the people seriously, including their own. 3) The priests modeled disrespect toward God instead of leading the people to worship God with all their heart, thus rejecting the very purpose for their role in the community.*

⭐ Why do you think God cares so much about our finances? What do our finances reveal about our hearts? *1) Where our treasure is, there our heart will be also (Matt. 6:21). 2) The love of money is the root of all kinds of evil (1 Tim. 6:10). 3) Whether hoarding money or demonstrating generosity, the way we treat money shows how much the gospel has captivated our hearts.*

⭐ Why is it fitting that the entire Old Testament closes with the threat of a curse? *1) The Old Testament points forward to the coming Christ but gives no power for keeping the law, so all stand condemned under the curse of the law. 2) No one is able to stand as righteous before God, and only a curse awaits those who try to do so by keeping the law. 3) The blessing of God comes not through the old covenant law but through the new covenant of grace established by Jesus in His death and resurrection.*

Our Mission

🔻 What do we communicate about our view of God and His grace toward us when we fail to give Him our very best? *God calls us to give the very best of everything we have out of love for Him. In fact, Scripture teaches that followers of Christ should be in the habit of offering up these five things in particular: our bodies (Rom. 12:1-2), our finances (Phil. 4:14-18), our praise (Heb. 13:15), our works (Heb. 13:16), and our witness (Rom. 15:16). In light of God's greatness and everything He freely offers to us through His Son, we should be willing to joyfully submit all things to Him in response.*

Pray

Close your group in prayer, asking God to make you aware of your own halfhearted worship and need for Jesus day by day.

THE CULMINATION OF REDEMPTION...

After 400 years of silence, God's promise to send a Rescuer comes to fulfillment in the life, death, and resurrection of Jesus Christ.

www.lifeway.com/gospelfoundations

GROUP DIRECTORY

Name: _____

Mobile Phone: _____

Email: _____

Social Media: _____

Name: _____

Mobile Phone: _____

Email: _____

Social Media: _____

Name: _____

Mobile Phone: _____

Email: _____

Social Media: _____

Name: _____

Mobile Phone: _____

Email: _____

Social Media: _____

Name: _____

Mobile Phone: _____

Email: _____

Social Media: _____

Name: _____

Mobile Phone: _____

Email: _____

Social Media: _____

Name: _____

Mobile Phone: _____

Email: _____

Social Media: _____

Name: _____

Mobile Phone: _____

Email: _____

Social Media: _____

Name: _____

Mobile Phone: _____

Email: _____

Social Media: _____

Name: _____

Mobile Phone: _____

Email: _____

Social Media: _____

Name: _____

Mobile Phone: _____

Email: _____

Social Media: _____

Name: _____

Mobile Phone: _____

Email: _____

Social Media: _____

Name: _____

Mobile Phone: _____

Email: _____

Social Media: _____

Name: _____

Mobile Phone: _____

Email: _____

Social Media: _____